MUSIC TEACHING FOR SPECIAL EDUCATIONAL NEEDS

A GUIDE FOR INSTRUMENTAL TEACHERS

Music Teaching
for Special Educational Needs

A Guide for Instrumental Teachers

David Baker

Acknowledgements

My heartfelt gratitude goes to the instrumental teachers and learners consulted during the production of this book, some of whom are now longstanding friends from my earlier Arts and Humanities Research Council 'Visually impaired musicians' lives' research (2013–15). Their perspectives as 'insiders' on SEND were essential for producing a practical guide. I am also grateful for the expertise and advice of: Lisa Carlin; Dr Kristl Kirk, Music Committee, British Dyslexia Association; Jay Pocknell, Music Support Officer, Royal National Institute of Blind People; James Risdon, Access Lead, Associated Board of the Royal Schools of Music; Joey Stuckey; and Dr Eunice Sin Ying Tang, Lecturer, Trinity Laban Conservatoire of Music and Dance. Thuy Hoang was also tremendously helpful. She read chapter drafts and commented from her perspective as an instrumental teacher working with children with ASD. I am also indebted to the published researchers and writers on SEND and pedagogy that are referenced in this book. Finally, my huge appreciation also goes to Lesley Rutherford, Publishing Director at Faber Music, and Rebecca Castell and Imogen Hall, Editors, for their guidance.

I am very fortunate to meet instrumental and class music teachers, and aspiring ones, each year from across the world. They come to University College London's Institute of Education to study and constantly remind me of the great importance of social justice and inclusion in music for learners with SEND. Leading UCL's Music Education MA course, with its extensive alumni network of music educators, has inspired me to write this book. I hope it will contribute to wider access to instrumental learning, and better experiences of it.

Contents

1

Introduction: Foundations for Understanding Special Educational Needs and Disabilities

This initial chapter lays essential groundwork for instrumental teachers' understanding of the subsequent ones. In this chapter, the terms 'disability' and 'Specific Learning Difficulty' are first defined and contrasted, as there is clarification of what is meant by Special Educational Needs and Disabilities (SEND). Then, the causes and categories of disabilities are discussed. Contextualising statistics on SEND are consequently provided, and there is discussion of where music participants are to be found, including within educational settings. The notion of an additional need is then introduced. The chapter subsequently turns to the medical and social models of disability to explain how our thinking on education, music education and music in society has changed towards a more socially just, inclusive view. This is particularly germane given most instrumental teachers will champion the wide-ranging benefits of music and notion of music for all. Building on this, attention is turned to apt terminology to describe people with disabilities. Pondering terms is significant for the instrumental teacher both to communicate with learners and their caregivers without causing offence, and to understand their lives and the issues within them. Throughout this book, all instances of 'parent' should be read as 'parent or guardian', reflecting the range of caregivers involved in supporting a learner. Unsurprisingly, teaching learners with SEND presents challenges too, but also some very exciting prospects, not least for the instrumental teacher's development. The chapter culminates by considering this. Threaded into the overall discussion are some general considerations for the instrumental teacher in shaping his or her future practices and thinking. As with the other chapters, several reflective questions are presented at its end to encourage the reader's contemplation. Further reading is also suggested for those who wish to pursue topics in greater depth.

A note on the structure and tone of this book

After laying foundations with Chapter 1, subsequent chapters (Chapters 2–6) focus on a specific disability or SpLD (specific learning difficulty). Each chapter includes pedagogical advice generated through a synthesis of published scholarship and refereed research, and illustrative teaching case studies. Most were founded on observational research in educational settings[1] understood through thematic analysis.[2] By drawing on the author's established network, it was possible to observe instrumental teachers and their pupils working together, make notes and interview the former.[3] Some of the music educators also identified themselves as a disabled person or had an SpLD. This meant they were able to articulate their 'insider' experiences as a music learner as well. For confidentiality, participants have been given pseudonyms, the names and locations of schools withheld, and other identifying features removed. Some of the pedagogical themes on visual disabilities (Chapter 4) also derive from the author's earlier 'Visually impaired musicians' lives' project, 2013–15, which was funded by the Arts and Humanities Research Council.[4] Chapter 7 concludes the book by asking 'What are the hallmarks of a good instrumental teacher?'

Be sceptical of pre-packaged, reportedly 'correct' instrumental pedagogies

SEND refers to an immeasurable array of different conditions, comorbidities (i.e., co-occurring health circumstances) and situations. This is duly reinforced at various points in this book. Within people defined as having visual impairments (i.e., those blind and partially sighted), just as one example, there will be *various* eye health conditions, visual acuity, visual fields and functional vision levels (if there is any), accessible learning materials possible and assistive technologies used (if at all). Consequently, there will be

---

1 see Foster, 1996; Jorgensen, 1989, 2020; Smart, Peggs & Burridge, 2013
2 Braun & Clarke, 2021
3 Flick, 2022; Gubrium et al., 2012; King, Horrocks & Brooks, 2019; Wengraf, 2001
4 Baker & Green, 2017

different ways of apprehending the world and learning music. On top of this, each person will have unique life experiences and educational aspirations in relation to music. Moreover, there are possible comorbidities. The person with a visual impairment may also have co-occurring conditions, for instance Autism Spectrum Disorder (ASD). So, if you have met one person who is visually impaired, you have met *one* person! The same applies equally to every classification of SEND. The effects on instrumental teaching and learning are infinite. Pedagogies should start from the learner's circumstances. A one-size-fits-all 'pedagogical toolkit' applicable to every learner within a particular disability or SpLD category is unachievable. It is unreasonable to expect this pre-packaged, supposedly 'correct' knowledge. That is the candid reality and not a weakness of this book. So, we ought to be dubious of professed 'experts' espousing some form of singularity. Instead, this book's purpose is to make instrumental teachers contemplate deeply the issues surrounding SEND and, with Chapters 2–6, to offer helpful pedagogical starting points only. These will have different emphases for individual students hence the cautious language readers may notice such as 'might be', 'may', etc. The worthiness of these teaching ideas can be reflected upon and tested in situ to develop apt strategies for specific music learners over time (also see Chapter 7 on 'reflective practice').

Understanding the terms SEND, disability and SpLD

Special Educational Needs and Disabilities (SEND)

'Special Educational Needs and Disabilities' (or SEND) is a commonplace term in UK education that encompasses *both* children with *disabilities* and learning *difficulties*. It is important for the instrumental teacher to understand that these two are different. SEND is used in schools to refer to learners who are formally identified as requiring additional support compared to their peers, or who have a Special Educational Need (SEN), due to a range of disability and neurodiversity conditions.

Disabilities

The World Health Organization[5] has developed an International Classification of Functioning (ICF) that details a *biopsychosocial* view of disability. This sees disability as the result of combined biological, psychological and social factors. The *biological dimension* relates to the functioning of the anatomical parts of a person's body (including the visible parts, but also the brain and nervous system), which adversely affect his or her ability, for example, to carry out commonplace tasks for daily living, or, indeed, to undertake those activities required within education and learning situations. The social dimension relates to unintentional or imposed restrictions resulting, for example, from other's attitudes and how they feed, as examples, an inaccessible built environment, education system or workplace. The *psychological dimension* relate, for example, to the person's experiences resulting from his or her body, this aforesaid social dimension, and what this means e.g., for confidence, self-esteem, or mental health. I unpack causes and categories of disabilities below.

Specific Learning Difficulties (SpLDs)

'Specific Learning Difficulties' (or SpLDs) are a set of diagnosable neurodiversity differences that affect individuals' information processing and learning. They include ADHD (Attention Deficit Hyperactivity Disorder), dyscalculia (affecting mathematical skills), dysgraphia (affecting e.g., handwriting), dyslexia (affecting word reading and spelling) and dyspraxia (affecting motor tasks, physical organisation and spatial awareness).

Learning *difficulties* versus learning *disabilities*

An important distinction must be made between, on the one hand, 'learning *difficulties*' and, on the other, 'learning *disabilities*'. There are instrumental learners with SpLDs who experience challenges

---

5 WHO, 2002

with aspects of learning yet, with the right support, have equivalent, or even higher, potential to achieve educationally as others. A key distinguishing factor is that their overall intellectual capacity and educational potential are not seen as insurmountably weaker or impaired. So, for example, a person with dyslexia may experience difficulties with reading a score (the music signs, symbols and text) but he or she may well be above average intelligence. With appropriate support too, he or she can have high attainment educationally, including in music. 'Learning *disability*', by contrast, refers to a significant intellectual impairment that means, regardless of any educational actions or adjustments, the person cannot achieve on par with whatever is deemed the normal attainment range by society. An example of this would be a person with Down Syndrome. For these reasons, some do not like SpLDs to be characterised as a disability at all. Accordingly, the term 'Specific Learning *Disability*' is avoided in this book.

Comorbidities

'Comorbidity' refers to the simultaneous occurrence of two or more conditions. So, for instance, a person may be a wheelchair user alongside ASD and an SpLD.

The causes and categories of disabilities

Causes

Some disabilities are caused by *genes*. They are, therefore, related hereditary characteristics passed from parents. Some example disabilities in this category are ocular albinism, muscular dystrophy and cystic fibrosis. Although we are not characterising them as disabilities, there is also some evidence that SpLDs have hereditary causes.[6] *Environmental* events cause disabilities too. These can include having an accident which then results in the person suddenly becoming a wheelchair user or losing his or her sight.

---

6 e.g., Shaywitz, Shaywitz, Fletcher & Escobar, 1990

Alternatively, a person might encounter an infectious disease that causes bodily damage (such as meningitis, leading to a serious intellectual disability). The natural process of *ageing* is also a cause of disability. Our bodies deteriorate over time. Examples of this are age-related macular degeneration (or AMD) which affects people's sight in later life, even arthritis, or, indeed, the natural deterioration of our cognitive capacities in old age. It is also worthwhile noting that the causes are sometimes *unknown* and mysterious.

Disability can be *non-discrete* too with complex interactions. A person's genetics, as an example, can affect his or her response to environmental factors, *or* how he or she ages, *or both*. For example, genetics can mean that, as a person ages, he or she responds less well to a poor diet (an environmental factor), has a stroke (causing a physical disability), and/or he or she develops diabetes (leading to a sensory issue, such as sight loss). Having a disability can equate to a variety of comorbidities. A good illustration is a person with Profound and Multiple Learning Disabilities (PMLDs). PMLD refers to having an intellectual disability along with another disability, or disabilities, such that communication, independence in daily living, and learning, are significantly impacted. Again, SpLDs, although not disabilities per se, have been found to have co-occurring conditions influencing music learning (see Rose, 2009).

Categories of disability

Disabilities have been categorised variously. However, we might understand them as sensory, physical, neurological, cognitive, intellectual and psychiatric.

Sensory disabilities impact hearing, touch and vision. As described later in this book, these affect how learners communicate with their instrumental teachers, the person's suitability for specific music learning processes or for certain instruments, and they may affect the materials they use too (for example, score types, or any assistive devices and technologies utilised for music-making).

Physical disabilities concern the absence of a body part, poor development of it, and/or inability to use it properly, including issues with the upper and lower body, the musculoskeletal or respiratory systems. These, again, will have a bearing on instrumental learning as discussed later.

By distinction, *neurological* disabilities are more specifically about the functioning of the brain, spinal cord and nervous system, which then have adverse effects on bodily movement. This can involve muscular weakness, sensitivity, numbness, or even affect speech and breathing. Both physical and neurological disabilities may impinge on an instrumental learner's capacity to manipulate a musical instrument too (for example, to strike a drum with an accurate rhythm or to place their fingers correctly on a guitar fretboard) and, therefore, the development of technical skills.

Cognitive disabilities affect how a person perceives and understands the world around him- or herself. These disabilities can range widely from potentially surmountable effects on music reading to more significant issues preventing any reading.

Intellectual disabilities affect thought processes, such as judgment and problem-solving, memory, communication and learning. We should bear in mind how much within instrumental learning is about the learner's judgment (such as what is accurate or not in performances, or acceptable or otherwise musically), or about memory (for example, musical signs and symbols, or of procedural information central to performing), or about the obvious matter of effective communication between the teacher and learner.

Finally, *psychiatric* disabilities are concerned with a person's emotions, including how his or her thought processes in that regard affect his or her behaviours.

When does disability occur?

We might also consider the point a disability happens and how long it lasts. The term 'congenital disability' refers to a condition that occurs in the pre-natal child or in the first months of life (such as Down syndrome, cerebral palsy). However, disabilities are not always something with which a person is born. Disability can be *lifelong*, but it can also arise at a later point in life making the person's instrumental learning experiences vastly different. Consider how different they would be for someone, on one hand, who is congenitally blind and learned to read music braille as a child (see Chapter 4) and, on the other, a stave notation reader who loses his or her sight in midlife. Learning music braille is neither quick nor easy. Aside from the potential for a disability to be congenital and lifelong, or to occur at a later point, it can also be *episodic*, as in some mental health conditions. A person may find him- or herself swinging between good and poor mental wellbeing dependent on medical interventions and pressures in life. This might affect the regularity of his or her instrumental lessons, changing their aims, or even envisioning them as respite and a helpful way to reduce pressures.

Table 1 provides a review of the disability causes and categories.

Table 1. Causes and categories of disabilities

Causes	*Discrete or interacting?*
Genetic	Genes and hereditary characteristics
Environmental	Injury, disease, infection
Ageing	Ageing, deterioration of the body
Unknown	*Mysterious causes*
Categories	*Episodic or lifelong?* *Congenital or appearing later in life?* *Obvious, hidden or undiagnosed?*
Sensory	About the senses of hearing, vision or touch
Physical	About the use of a body part, including the musculoskeletal and respiratory systems (or the absence or incomplete development of a body part)
Neurological	About the nervous system (brain, spinal cord and nerves) with potential effects, including on bodily movement or muscular weakness, issues with sensitivity or numbness, or on speech and breathing

Cognitive	About how a person perceives and understands
Intellectual	About thought processes affecting i.e., problem-solving, judgment, memory, communication and learning
Psychiatric	About a person's emotions and thought processes adversely affecting behaviours

There are three common teacher misconceptions that I have come across. These are detailed in Table 2 below. Each will be addressed in turn.

Table 2. Some common misconceptions of instrumental teachers

Misconception
1   I've never come across an instrumental student with SEND.
2   The number of people with SEND is far too low to be concerned with them as instrumental learners.
3   Disabled children are educated in special schools, so in the mainstream schools where I teach, I will not come across them.

Sadly, I have heard in-service and trainee music teachers remark, 'I've never come across an instrumental student with SEND'. This is **Misconception 1**. Both disabilities and SpLDs can go *undiagnosed*, which is a sobering thought for an instrumental teacher encountering large volumes of learners across his or her career. They can also be purposefully *hidden*, perhaps due to the person's fear of stigma[7] and anticipation of negative consequences. Instrumental teachers must remain vigilant for the signs, therefore. SEND conditions can also be hidden simply because they are less easily observed. Whereas a wheelchair user is more easily *seen* to be disabled, that is not the case for someone with, for example, a discrete hearing aid, prosthetic leg, poor vision, dyslexia or an implant.

---

7 Jones, 1972

How many people are there with SEND? Where are they?

Another misconception is 'The number of people with SEND is far too low to be concerned with them as instrumental learners' (*Misconception 2*). On the contrary, if we *both* understand instrumental learning to be a meaningful part of lifelong experience *and* account for SEND in all its manifestations, this is awry. Worldwide, there are many people to consider when we adopt an inclusive vision as instrumental teachers. The World Health Organization estimates there are 1.3 billion people who experience significant disability representing 16% of the world's population.[8] WHO equates this to 1 in 6 people globally with prevalence increasing by age. The United Nations Children's Fund reports that, globally, 1 in 10 children up to the age of 17 years has a disability.[9]

There are some cautions, however, when considering statistics on disability. Per capita numbers in particular countries, for instance, will vary according to poverty levels, health influenced by poor living conditions, differences in healthcare systems, diagnosis rates and, ultimately, what 'counts' as a disability. So, developing countries will have different rates to those with stronger economies. Additionally, any national or world statistics take considerable time to collect and compile so surveys are, inevitably, dated when published. Then there are undiagnosed and hidden conditions, as described earlier, whereby statistics may underestimate levels. Conversely, there is chance some stakeholder charities may overestimate in their projections to garner funding.

Disabilities are not just widespread in the developing world. National surveys from developed countries also show substantial levels. A research report for the UK Parliament's House of Commons Library has estimated that 16.1 million people had a disability in the 2022–23 financial year, or 24% of the UK population.[10] Based on the American Community Survey, the United States Census Bureau found that, in 2021, approximately 42.5 million people (or 13%) among the US population had a disability, with higher rates in rural residents.[11] There are similarly large numbers in other

---

8 WHO, 2022   9 UNICEF, 2021   10 Kirk-Wade, Stiebahl & Wong, 2024   11 Crankshaw, 2023

countries i.e., where sophisticated healthcare systems exist to identify disabilities with researchers subsequently capturing and reporting the information. Similarly, if we consider an SpLD, the British Dyslexia Association (BDA) estimates that approximately 10% of the UK population has the condition.[12] So, there are undoubtedly many children and adults with SEND in our communities. They may wish to learn a musical instrument or may already be learning one.

Some UK instrumental teachers visit mainstream schools (known as 'public schools' in the US) each day for their employment. I have heard several of these peripatetic instrumental teachers remark, 'Disabled children are educated in special schools, so in the mainstream schools where I teach, I will not come across them' (this is *Misconception 3*). Quite the opposite: they are likely to be encountered. Government policies in developed countries have been to educate disabled students in mainstream schools alongside their non-disabled peers where feasible. This has placed a responsibility on schools and educators to make reasonable adjustments in support of learning (see e.g., the Special Educational Needs and Disability Act 2001 in the UK, or the Individuals with Disability Education Act, 1997, 2004 in the US). Under these policies, educating disabled children in mainstream schools is seen to have benefits for social adjustment and inclusion.

In 2023–24, there were 9.1 million children in English schools overall.[13] In the same year, the UK government reported that there were over 1.6 million pupils in England alone with a Special Educational Need (SEN).[14] So, this means that approximately 18% of the overall English school population had a one, which includes children with disabilities and SpLDs. Most of them attended a mainstream school. Only 161,072 of the children with a SEN (about 1%) attended a special school.[15] In the US, as another example, the National Center for Education Statistics noted that, in 2022–23, the number of public (mainstream) school students of 3–21 years who received special education services was 7.5 million, or 15% of all students.[16] So, just by looking at these two countries, we can see

---

12 BDA, 2025   13 Gov.uk, 2024a   14 Gov.uk, 2024b   15 UK Parliament, 2024
16 NCES, 2024

that the numbers are significant. It is sensible to assume that some of those same children will wish to have instrumental lessons either within or outside their school setting; some will already be doing so.

Additional needs

The terms 'Special Educational Needs' (SEN), 'additional needs' and 'reasonable adjustments' are used in connection with learners with SEND. An additional need occurs when a pupil's learning cannot occur effectively through, for example, strategies and resources that are customarily effective. However, catering for additional needs in instrumental studies is not merely about teaching practices and the training of those who deliver them. We need to be mindful not only to consider what happens in the teaching room, or to focus solely on its physical environment (such as access for wheelchairs, trip hazards or installed induction loops for hearing aids, etc.). Those are, indeed, important, but there are broader matters such as the instrumental learner's background, the approaches to music-making he or she has encountered (and the associated materials), or even his or her confidence, etc. There are also aspects of resourcing on which to reflect (funding for assistive devices for music, acquiring required score formats, etc.). Moreover, travel to lessons and a person's mobility can have significant implications. Mobility lies on a spectrum, from being entirely dependent on caregivers to entirely independent, and it might incur additional costs for the learner. After all, access to a musical experience relies on getting to it. Table 3 offers some reflections on key areas of additional needs.

Table 3. Some reflection on additional needs

Item	Reflections
Aims	The aims of the learning will depend on the learner's health condition, capacities and the preferences of those involved. They will be negotiated with people, but also consider the expectations of the

	learning context, e.g., that of an education system or school, or the arrangements for private instruction, etc.
Pedagogical practices	Practices will be altered in e.g., the structure and organisation of lessons, interactions, materials, language use, how assessment is arranged, etc.
Materials	Materials may need to be reconsidered, e.g., by offering alternative score formats, or by not using scores, etc.
Assistive technologies	Learners may need e.g., instrument adaptations, or appropriate hearing aids, magnification, braille devices, or software, etc.
Physical environment	The suitability of the teaching space will need consideration, including e.g., its acoustics, light, the arrangement of people within it, installed equipment, such as induction loops for hearing aids, step-free access, etc.
Mobility	The learner's mobility will be on a spectrum ranging from entirely independent to highly dependent subject to his or her health condition, background and confidence. This will affect travel to lessons.
Support	Various levels of support may be needed, e.g., scribes or readers for examinations, other examination adjustments, sighted guides, parental involvement in lessons, etc.
Time	Additional time may be required to learn due to the student's health, the nature of the materials and the adjusted approach. There may also be time pressures

	impacting music learning from elsewhere, e.g., from daily living or the learning of other subjects.
Learner background	It will be important to account for the learner's prior musical experiences and approaches, as well as his or her life, wider educational experiences and resultant confidence.
Costs	Adapted equipment for music, assistive technologies, supported travel, etc. may incur additional costs.

Some considerations for the instrumental teacher
(interim summary):

- *Investigate* the nature of the learner's SEND condition. Visit the websites of official medical organisations and any national charities concerned with it. *Identify* any music advisory services within the latter.
- *Discuss* with learners, where possible, and/or their caregivers any successful and unsuccessful prior musical experiences. Be aware that the point at which a disability occurs, and its duration, significantly affects music learning experiences.
- *Reflect* that additional needs are not about teaching strategies and learning materials alone. Ponder how learning is affected by the lesson space, access to it, the learner's level of dependence on travel and on carers, and any extra costs incurred, etc.

Inclusion and the social model of disability

From the 1960s, new thinking on disability emerged. This was known as 'the social model'. Advocates argued that it was unfair to blame a supposedly 'atypical' or 'faulty' body for the challenges confronting a disabled person (the earlier 'medical model'). Instead, these were caused by society's poor organisation in its physical environment, attitudes, policy, resources and funding, etc. Rather than people with disabilities being framed as somehow 'defective' and, accordingly, solely responsible for adapting and fitting in, they were to be understood as part of humanity's typical spectrum. In this way, disabilities were normalised. An emphasis was, therefore, placed on putting in place steps to reduce their problems. Put another way, if society was set up to be accessible, disabled people would not be excluded or restricted. Today, in many countries, this has driven policies and laws leading to helpful adaptations to the physical environment (such as wheelchair ramps, induction loops for hearing aids, braille signage, etc.). It has also led to support mechanisms and reasonable adjustments within institutions in schools, universities and elsewhere. It has been a move towards an inclusive view of disabled people.

This makes sense. Nearly every person will be disabled, including you and me, unless our lives are cut short by a serious accident or sudden illness. If not an officially diagnosed, undiagnosed or a hidden disability, we will likely encounter physical and cognitive deterioration in old age. It is to be expected. So, disability is the norm not the anomaly. It seems peculiar, then, to package and refer to disabled people as an exclusive group – a matter of 'them' (who must adapt) and 'us' (who have no need). Most instrumental teachers will surely wish to include the entire spectrum of society in their learner market, that is, to include people with and without a SEND or disability, younger and older people, and so forth.

Even though many governments and organisations now advocate the social model, or aspects thereof, regrettably, there can be gaps between policy and practice. Many instrumental music teachers lack pedagogical training and knowledge, let alone in relation to SEND.

In a research study of 61 undergraduates at a leading UK music conservatoire, Janet Mills (2004a) found that 77% of the participants had already taught music before commencing their studies.

It is understandable, therefore, that many instrumental teachers do not know where to go for key resources in relation to SEND (such as adapted scores, assistive technologies, etc.). Assistive devices and software technologies for music can be expensive and hard for learners or their caregivers to acquire, that is, assuming they are informed and kept abreast of the possibilities. With music learning, unfortunately, much is left to enthusiastic educators to find answers or to avid music representatives in stakeholder charities (such as in the UK, the music team of the Royal National Institute of Blind People, the Music of Life Foundation, the Amber Trust, the National Deaf Children's Society, etc.).

Describing disabled music learners appropriately

The social model also led to more appropriate, inclusive language for describing disabled people. You might think this is all an unnecessary fuss and inconsequential, but, for the instrumental music teacher, pondering it deeply is helpful for appreciating the circumstances and issues of disabled people's lives. It is essential not to cause offence too. However, it is important to note that there are many contrasting views on the right terms, even amongst disabled people themselves, between stakeholder organisations worldwide and between different medical systems internationally. So, selecting the most appropriate language is really a matter *both* of respecting the context within which you are operating *and* honouring the wishes of disabled instrumental learners themselves and/or their caregivers (e.g., of family members or other professionals working with them). The best advice is to be frank and have conversations about preferred terminology. Below is some advice drawing on some current thinking and policy:

Avoiding language that evokes helplessness, pity and negativity

It is important to avoid language that reinforces helplessness such as 'wheelchair bound' or 'handicapped'. The latter evokes someone holding a cap in his or her hand who must beg. Better terms are e.g., a 'person who uses a wheelchair' or a 'disabled person'. It is prudent to avoid terms that evoke pity too, such as 'stricken by', 'afflicted by', 'troubled with' or 'suffering from'. Terms that emphasise abnormality in relation to disabled people should also be avoided such as 'disorder', 'invalid' (about validity as a member of society), or 'the able-bodied' (a generalisation implying that no disabled person can use his or her body well). More appropriate language is 'a person with a physical disability'.

Person-first and identity-first language

Contrasting positions exist concerning person- versus identity-first language. Person-first language means putting the person first, so 'person with a disability', or 'people with a hearing impairment' rather than its identity-first counterpart, 'disabled person'. The reasoning here is that, through the person-first approach, we focus on the human being rather than defining him or her by the disability.[17] The United Nations favours this.[18] Contrariwise, those who favour an identity-first approach[19] argue that 'disabled person' more clearly indicates not so much that the person has a disability, but, instead, has been disabled by society.[20]

Impairments and deficits

Another consideration is about how the words we select reinforce deficits or what a person *cannot do*. Terms like 'impairment', as in 'hearing impaired', 'visually impaired', or *dis*-abled' emphasise that a person has a deficit in their functioning, and is therefore different, or abnormal. Some question this. Nonetheless, such terms are used widely, for example, in medical systems. For example, the UK's National Health Service divides people who are 'visually impaired' (to include people registered as blind or partially sighted) into sub-categories of 'sight impaired' and 'severely sight impaired'.[21]

d/Deaf

We should also reflect on the terms used for d/Deaf people. The World Health Organization states that anyone who cannot hear

---

17 also see Kenny et al., 2016 on debates in relation to autism   18 UN, 2024
19 Disability Wales, 2024   20 Disability Rights UK, 2024   21 NHS, 2021

sound below a threshold of 20 dB has 'hearing *loss*'.[22] This can range from less to more substantial impacts. 'Loss' is a misnomer, however, in the case of people who have had a stable condition of impeded or no hearing since birth. According to the WHO (ibid.), 'deaf' is reserved for more profound hearing loss conditions, that is, with little or no sensation of sound through the auditory system. In another approach, the UK charity SignHealth (2024) offers that 'deaf', with a lowercase 'd', denotes someone with limited hearing due to adventitious causes (for example, through illness, accidents or old age). 'Deaf' with a capital 'D' is reserved for people who have had their condition throughout their lives and before they learned to talk (that is, pre-lingually). The British Academy of Audiology (2024) continues that people who identify as 'Deaf' mostly use British Sign Language (BSL) (with those in other countries using their counterpart sign languages e.g., US American Sign Language [ASL]). Signing is seen as the primary, or first, language. Thus, 'deaf' and 'Deaf' indicate two groups with distinct health and perceptual circumstances but also two social groups. Indeed, a distinction is sometimes drawn between 'members of a hearing culture' who can communicate through spoken language, and 'members of a deaf culture' who are largely sign language users.[23]

Table 4. Considering terminology and disability

Consider	*Avoid*
disabled person, person with a disability	*the* disabled (othering), handicapped, atypical, differently abled
non-disabled person, person without a disability	normal, typical
person with an intellectual disability/impairment	retarded, simple, slow, intellectually challenged, feeble-minded, imbecile

---

22 WHO, 2024   **23** Darrow, 1993

person with a psychiatric disability	lunatic, demented, maniac, mentally deranged, mentally defective
d/Deaf person, person who is deaf, person who is Deaf, person with a hearing disability/impairment	*the* deaf, deaf and dumb
visually impaired person, person who is visually impaired, person who is blind, person who is partially sighted, person who is sight impaired, person who is severely sight impaired	*the* blind
person with a physical disability/impairment	cripple, invalid, deformed, handicapped, physically challenged person
person without a physical disability/impairment	able-bodied
wheelchair user, person who uses a wheelchair, person with a mobility impairment	confined to a wheelchair, wheelchair bound
person with a [condition/ disability]	victim of, stricken by, afflicted by, troubled with, suffering from, etc.
person with dyslexia, learner with dyslexia	a dyslexic person, dyslexic learner
Specific Learning Difficulty	Specific Learning Disability

Terms used in this book

In this book, both person- and identity-first language, such as 'disabled person' and 'person with a disability', is used. Similarly, terms such as 'person with a physical impairment' or 'visually impaired' are employed. This is simply because these are commonplace, accepted within some organisations and medical systems, and widely understood. The term 'Specific Learning *Difficulty*' (rather than 'Specific Learning *Disability*') is also used, certainly not to downplay the gravity of an SpLD, but because this is commonplace in the UK. Regardless, deep consideration of the meanings underlying words is very helpful for instrumental teachers. It helps us to be more thoughtful and empathetic regarding learners with SEND. Table 4 provides a starting point for contemplation. The need for empathy in instrumental teaching is revisited in Chapter 7.

Some considerations for the instrumental teacher
(interim summary):

- *Ponder* how we might best describe people with SEND, as this allows us to be sensitive, avoid offence and understand their life circumstances.
- *Identify* and familiarise yourself with the language used in your professional context and, where viable, ask disabled learners and their caregivers.

Some key challenges for the instrumental teacher

Teaching instrumental learners with SEND presents music educators with understandable challenges. However, without some obstacles to surmount, teaching rapidly becomes monotonous, so this should not be framed negatively as 'a problem'. When the teacher sees him- or herself as a lifelong learner[24] and reflective practitioner[25] (see Chapter 8), this leads to exciting new avenues.

Pedagogical approaches and materials

Firstly, there is the matter of *pedagogical approaches and materials*. Learners with SEND may have specific requirements entailing pedagogical methods, materials, assistive software and devices of which the teacher is unaccustomed. Learners with visual disabilities,

---

24 Roulston, 2010   25 Dewey, 1933; Schön, 1992

as one example, might use adapted scores (large print or modified stave notation, or braille, etc.) sometimes in conjunction with assistive technology devices for their daily living and/or music, or they might not use notation at all. Or the visually impaired person may have no music learning experience at all and no understanding of possible approaches. As another example, there may be a 'learning curve' for the instrumental teacher when adjusting his or her pedagogy or adapting scores successfully for learners with SpLDs. Since individuals with SEND will have needs that vary widely, including them in any group music teaching will necessitate careful thought on differentiation, and sometimes even a significant shift in overall approach.

Suitable aims

Secondly, there is the matter of *suitable aims*. The nature of a learner's condition raises a weighty question about this, which instrumental teachers need to ponder very carefully. SpLDs and some disability circumstances neither preclude learning an instrument from some form of notation (even stave scores) nor prevent learning through an examination system that is the teacher's norm (e.g., Associated Board of the Royal Schools of Music grades). With other circumstances however, aural learning approaches (for example, by ear, without notation) might be more practical. Furthermore, for instrumental teachers working with groups or ensembles, there may be a choice to be made between what Thomas Turino (2008) calls 'presentational' and 'participatory' music (see Table 5). This might be, for example, due to the range of health circumstances included in a differentiated group, or the connotations of, for instance, intellectual disabilities for accessing standard notation in the usual way.

'Presentational music' is scripted. Performers read a music score produced by a composer i.e., in stave notation. So, the composer is often separate from its performer with the latter a conduit for his or her intentions. The piece is known to the performer or performers ahead of time as it is rehearsed. It requires generous technical skills to execute. Those of us who have learned through the lens of classical music will likely recognise this. With 'participatory music', by distinction, the group participants *are* the composers. It is potentially made by those of a wide variety of technical skill levels. It entails improvised forms, typically without any notation or the necessity to be able to read a score. Its final product, beginnings and endings are unscripted. Critically, it aims not for high technical competence and the delivery of an esteemed heritage repertoire. Instead, it is about enjoyment, aesthetic awareness, building a sense of community and social inclusion. This participatory view has been significant in the aural traditions of world music and community music practice.[26] Keith Swanwick (2011) writes:

> Musicians from outside western traditions are well aware . . . that musical fluency takes precedence over musical literacy. It is precisely fluency, the aural ability to image music coupled with the skill of handling an instrument (or the voice), that characterises jazz, Indian music, rock music, music for steel-pans, a great deal of computer-assisted music and folk music anywhere in the world. Notation of any kind has limited or no virtue for performers of Korean *sanjo*, or Texas-Mexican *conjunto* accordion music, or *salsa*, or Brazilian *capoeira*. These musicians have much to teach about the virtues of playing 'by ear' and of the possibilities of extended musical memory and collective improvisation (p. 77).

Even this participatory alternative may be entirely out of the question, for example, when addressing learners with PMLDs. Owing to considerable intellectual disabilities, social interaction and communication issues, the emphasis shifts again. Adam Ockelford (2000) remarks that, for those learners, music contributes to their wider development of bodily awareness and control, their communication skills through, for example, 'sound signals', and, moreover, 'music sessions offer a unique and secure framework through which many of the skills and disciplines of social interaction can be experienced and developed' (p. 212).

---

26 Bartleet & Higgins, 2018; Higgins, 2012, 2024

The Sounds of Intent framework maps the musical development of young people with complex needs like these.[27] The crux is that, under the hypernym SEND exists an expansive array of learner circumstances, capabilities and individual circumstances, which affect both how instrumental lessons are best taught and their aims.

Table 5. Presentational versus participatory music, adapted from Turino (2008)

Presentational (the classical music lens)	*Participatory* (*more akin to many genres of world music*)
Individual and ensemble performance	Group work
Scripted forms, music scores	Improvised forms, no score
Musical form predetermined, with a clear beginning and end	Musical form emerges, with a feathered beginning and ending
Scores rehearsed	No rehearsal
Composer and performer separate	Performers are the composers
Acquiring significant technical skills is required, coherent prior skills required of ensemble members	Participants can have diverse instrumental skills and backgrounds
Learning according to a 'staged' curriculum of repertoire of increasing difficulty	No formal curriculum
Aims of technical competence, acquiring and performing valued repertoire well, etc.	Aims of enjoyment through group interaction, social inclusion

27 see Sounds of Intent, 2025; Vovajolu & Ockelford, 2016; Welch et al., 2009

Training and awareness

Thirdly, there is *training and the instrumental teacher's awareness*. Available training for instrumental teachers about SEND is sometimes tokenistic, or even absent, in any courses they have received. It is often left to optional postgraduate study or in-service training. Instrumental teachers come from a culture of training and initiation that ascribes higher status to performance skills than pedagogic knowledge.[28] This is regrettable both considering the many identified benefits of musical participation for everyone from published research,[29] and the widespread support for educational inclusion in developed countries. Instrumental teachers are normally made responsible for acquiring information by exploring the webpages of health services and stakeholder charities, or he or she must read books such as this one on music pedagogy but after starting his or her career.

Constraints

Fourthly, there are *constraints on the instrumental teacher*. Instrumental teachers can be inhibited by where they work to some extent. The teaching context itself is an important consideration. It might be, for example, that a pressured, oversubscribed school does not have an entirely suitable teaching space for a disabled instrumental learner. A room might, for example, not have an induction loop for the student's hearing aid, or it might be next to a noisy, distracting classroom not best suited for a student with ADHD. Moreover, in the private teaching studio, some adaptations might be more possible than others. The teacher may also encounter contrasting attitudes from others within a teaching site itself, or from families and other caregivers. Those viewpoints might, for example, be about whether learning an instrument is viable, cost-effective and worthwhile for the student. Bear in mind that disabled learners and their families may already be under pressure from the additional costs incurred due to assisted

---

28 Boyle, 2020   **29** Hallam & Himonides, 2022

travel, purchasing expensive assistive devices, or where there are additional stresses and strains from a child's wider education (such as from the additional time needed for gaining daily living skills or to digest other school subjects).

Disclosure, sharing and awareness

Finally, there can be issues with *disclosure, sharing and awareness*. Some learners with SEND may be less willing to share information about their conditions and needs due to perceived stigma or even embarrassment. Moreover, schools might not wish to share pupils' SEND details, or overlook sharing them, with visiting instrumental specialists. Sometimes, this can largely result from practicalities i.e., because those peripatetic musicians typically dash in and out of various schools each day for short teaching slots. This is troubling, though, given the possibility of learner needs not being met. Issues with sharing information within educational sites may also be related to data protection legislation in particular countries. In the UK, for instance, the General Data Protection Regulations (GDPR) resulted from the Data Protection Act 2018.[30] GDPR sets out legal obligations for the storage and processing of people's personal data, including those of school-age learners, with 'health' and 'SEND' being special categories that schools are prohibited to process without special conditions.[31] Schools may, therefore, be understandably cautious.

Some considerations for the instrumental teacher
(interim summary):

- *Avoid* imposing a well-worn, single approach for learners with SEND used effectively with other students. Be open to considering alternative approaches and materials (e.g., available score types, assistive technologies, etc.).
- *Consider* how SEND affects the aims of learning music and a musical instrument.

---

30 Gov.uk, 2024c   **31** Gov.uk, 2024d, e

- *Advocate* for the worth of music for all. When teaching in educational and other sites, politely share where adaptations, adjustments and accessibility improvements are needed.
- *Approach* Special Educational Needs Coordinators (SENCos) in UK schools where you teach, or their counterparts in other countries. Discuss pupil needs and what information can be shared.

What are the opportunities?

A positive multidimensional framing of SEND

It is all too easy to conceptualise SEND as inherently negative i.e., something that 'impedes', 'affects', or 'prevents'. Although we do need to consider its effects *on* instrumental learning in terms of processes, materials, aims and pedagogies, etc., there can be a more positive, multidimensional framing. It is helpful to think about how learning can have potential health and welfare benefits *for* the disabled person, as well as considering the potential advantages of some neurodiversity traits *in* music learning. These will be touched upon in the ensuing chapters.

The instrumental teacher as 'explorer', 'advocate' and 'agent of social change'

Learners with SEND offer immensely exciting prospects. After many years, an instrumental teacher may believe he or she has 'all the answers' to situations encountered. This inevitably leads to a lacklustre career and feeling jaded. Developing a new client base, advancing new skills and understandings, and nurturing a meaningful 'specialism' is a constructive way to allay this. Some ways in which this might happen are explored in Chapter 7. Indeed, great opportunities exist for continuously cultivating and sharing better approaches as a practitioner. The teacher needs to be willing to discover new strategies by taking a different path. In that sense, he or she can be *an explorer*. In taking on that role, he or she can draw on available advice, test it, enjoy the satisfaction of surmounting challenges, and share and assist in pooling knowledge on 'what works' and 'what does not'. All this can potentially happen through conversations with likeminded colleagues in schools, music services or hubs, etc. Such dialogue is powerfully transformative both for the teacher's own personal development and wellbeing, but also for wider educational improvement.

Most instrumental teachers, too, will espouse that music can benefit anyone who wishes to engage. Understanding, pointing out and resolving shortfalls in the instrumental music provision for learners with SEND is also transformative. In that way, the instrumental teacher can be *an advocate*. It requires commitment and responsiveness to *every* learner. It fits well with the notion the 'virtuoso teacher' coined by Paul Harris (2015):

> Virtuoso teachers teach as the virtuoso player plays: with a heightened sense of awareness, with passion and energy, with profound involvement and genuine commitment. ... Virtuoso teachers are truly transformational – they can create the aspiration *in each of their pupils* to discover, explore and realise his or her own unlimited musical potential (pp. 7–8).

Clearly, the instrumental music teacher holds considerable power in his or her arsenal. Perhaps the most exciting prospect is adopting an inclusive, socially just worldview to drive practice. Through his or her love of music, both as an explorer and advocate, he or she has great potential to profoundly transform society for the better – as *an agent for social change*.

Reflective questions

- What is meant by SEND, disabilities and SpLDs?
- How might we categorise disabilities and what are their causes?
- What are the connotations of the language used to describe disabled instrumental learners? How might we best select terms?
- What are the challenges and opportunities when working with learners with SEND?

- How might aims and approaches shift according to the learner's specific circumstances?
- What is the instrumental teacher's role in aiding a more socially just society?

Suggested further reading

Carrico, A., & Grennell, K. (2024). *Disability and accessibility in the music classroom: A teacher's guide*. Routledge.

Crichton, L. (1992). Music for everyone? *British Journal of Music Education, 9*(3), 211–215.

Lerner, N., & Straus, J. N. (2007). *Sounding off: Theorising disability in music*. Routledge.

Lubet, A. (2011). *Music, disability, and society*. Temple University Press.

Oliver, M. (2009). *Understanding disability: From theory to practice*. Palgrave Macmillan.

Straus, J. N. (2011). *Extraordinary measures: Disability in music*. Oxford University Press.

Valle, J. W., & Connor, D. J. (2019). *Rethinking disability: A disability studies approach to inclusive practices*. Routledge.

Vargas, A. A. T. (2020). *Disability and music performance*. Routledge.

Wearmouth, J. (2023). *Special Educational Needs and Disability: The basics*. Routledge.

2

Dyslexia, as an Example
of a Specific Learning Difficulty

What is dyslexia?

Dyslexia falls within the group of conditions known as Specific Learning Difficulties (SpLDs) with others including dyscalculia, dysgraphia, dyspraxia and Attention Deficit Hyperactivity Disorder (ADHD) (also see Chapter 1). It is associated with difficulties e.g., in processing written language and music notation.[1] Dyslexia can result in significant challenges with reading comprehension, writing and spelling. Examples are mixing up multisyllabic words, spelling errors, missing out vowels, etc. There can be issues with phonological awareness (i.e., being able to segment a sentence into words, or words into syllables, or recognising alliterations or rhyme, etc.), verbal memory (e.g., struggling to recall words or storylines, etc.), and slow verbal processing speed.[2] There are persistent challenges for students with dyslexia despite pedagogical approaches and learning opportunities considered effective with others.[3]

Given parallels between verbal language and music, it is unsurprising that dyslexia needs careful consideration in instrumental teaching. It should be considered as multifaceted and a continuum however, and not a distinct, single, easily self-contained category. This is because it impacts individuals to various extents and in many ways. As Sheila Oglethorpe (2000) puts it, '. . . there must be as many variations of what we call dyslexia (or specific learning difficulties) as there are species of roses . . .' (p. 57). Significantly too, statistical research has revealed a significant prevalence of co-occurring conditions. Dyslexia and reading issues '. . . seem to co-exist most

---

1 Reid et al., 2008
2 see Rose, 2009; cf. Bryant & Bradley, 1985, Snowling, 1997 on a phonological deficit theory
3 Tunmer & Greaney, 2010

clearly with ADHD . . . and motor deficits . . .' as well as Autism Spectrum Disorder (ASD) (see Chapter 3).[4] This is not to suggest that every person with dyslexia will have a comorbidity.

Some research posits that dyslexia results from brain structure and connectivity differences in the left planum temporale, which is utilised for language and reading.[5] It has also been proposed that dyslexia occurs in 40–60% of children who have a parent with the condition.[6]

Dyslexia can be hidden and easily go unidentified for reasons discussed in Chapter 1. Heikkila and Knight (2012) propose various indicators of dyslexia linked to children's ages (see Table 6).

Table 6. Potential dyslexia indicators by age (Heikkila & Knight, 2012)

Area	*Preschool (2–4 years)*	*Early elementary/ primary (4–7 years)*	*Middle elementary/ primary (7–10 years)*
Speech	Delayed verbalisation	Problems differentiating 'switched' sounds or 'switching' sounds within words	Diagnosis of auditory processing disorder
Cognition	Impaired visual tracking	Difficulty reading and spelling, short-term memory issues	Difficulty reading and spelling
Physical	Reverse 'mirror' writing, delayed walking, motor skill deficits	Dysgraphia (difficulty writing or typing) or with other fine motor deficits	

---

4 Brimo et al. 2021, p. 279; also see Fawcett & Nicolson, 1995; Gillberg, 2010; Kaplan et al., 2001; Peterson & Pennington, 2015
5 see Galaburda & Kemper, 1979; Galaburda et al., 1985; Humphreys et al., 1990; Hoeft et al., 2006; Hynd et al., 1990; Larsen et al., 1990; Williams, Juranek, Cirino & Fletcher, 2018
6 Shaywitz, Shaywitz, Fletcher & Escobar, 1990

Dyslexia and intelligence

Unfortunately, dyslexia has been misunderstood as '. . . a "scapegoat" diagnosis for children who are seen as "less intelligent" than average'.[7] On the contrary, dyslexia occurs across a broad range of intellectual capabilities. People with average or above average intelligence can have it.[8] Since there is no evidence to suggest people with dyslexia are inherently below average intelligence, with suitable support learners may have potential for high achievement, musically or otherwise.

Dyslexia, music and an interesting alternative theory on timing

An interesting theory on dyslexia emerged in 2000. Katie Overy (2000) and others proposed that language and literacy problems were derived from neurological timing, or *temporal processing* issues. Overy contended that people with dyslexia struggle to pro-cess sensory information (that non-dyslexics can process more efficiently) when it enters the nervous system in rapid succession.

> *An interesting experiment was conducted by Tallal, Miller and Fitch (1993). In this, children were presented with two pitches, one higher, one lower, and they were asked whether the first was higher or lower. Their control group, i.e., without dyslexia, could consistently distinguish this at intervals of only 30ms (milliseconds). Those with a language difficulty struggled at much larger time intervals (of 350ms or more). The authors contend that this accounts for errors distinguishing between phonemes in the speech (e.g., between 'ba' and 'da') that occur at similarly rapid rates.*

The impacts on instrumental learning

There are obvious parallels between verbal language and music. Noting the effects of dyslexia on breaking down sounds into their component parts, on memory, and bearing in mind the additional

---

7 Heikkila & Knight, 2012, p. 54   **8** Vance, 2004

time needed to process information, dyslexia may result in notable challenges for the instrumental learner. Examples include obstacles related to:

- decoding the abstract symbols associated with stave music notation and music theory (e.g., identifying on which line a notehead is positioned, recognising melodic contour, grasping symbolic rhythmic information, etc.)
- note naming or understanding written performance directions on scores
- processing speed in relation to the above bullet points
- recalling melodic and/or rhythmic information, or musical concepts
- identifying (and breaking down) component melodic and/or rhythmic structures in a melody or piece
- sequencing (e.g., performing notes in the correct order, or following the order of instructions given by the teacher)
- sight-reading, including associated anxiety about it
- visual discomfort when reading music resulting in fatigue
- motor coordination (e.g., problems with fingerings or bowing, etc.)
- memory more generally e.g., in relation to remembering instructions in instrumental lessons or music examinations
- attention and concentration, both within instrumental lessons and in general personal organisation

Some of these are not essential markers for a dyslexia diagnosis (e.g., concentration, personal organisation) but are regularly co-occurring difficulties.[9] Certainly, dyslexia can result in anxiety, frustration and low self-esteem in the instrumental learner, particularly so when reading music. Teachers will sculpt their pedagogies more effectively by considering the implications for:

- Identifying and decoding
- Recalling

---

9 Rose, 2009

- Information processing speed
- Sequencing
- Memory
- Motor coordination
- Attention and concentration

The benefits of learning an instrument

Playing a musical instrument engages auditory, motor and spatial skills, so there are potential transferrable benefits for music learners with dyslexia. Owing both to its rhythmic content and the need to coordinate rhythmically with others, instruments provide a medium for practising fine timing skills, thus conceivably improving the temporal timing needed for language. Instrumental studies may also help with the learner's capacities at sequential activity, by improving visual tracking by reading scores, boosting the auditory perception required for reading and enhancing motor skills and finger dexterity for handwriting.[10] Additionally, musical engagement typically requires very high levels of attention and concentration and, therefore, assists the learner in being able to distinguish, for example, between conversation and background noise, to follow instructions and to improve his or her general self-organisation. For students with dyslexia, there can be great enjoyment too, a sense of inclusion and gains in confidence and self-esteem.

Pedagogy

General considerations in pedagogy

Individual and group lessons, and differentiation

Some writers have suggested that instrumental learners with dyslexia are best served by small-group and one-to-one private music instruction.[11] Their argument hinges on a stated need for individual attention and specific approaches. This may not be practical for the teacher who must integrate learners into larger shared or

---

10 Oglethorpe, 2008a   **11** Nelson & Hourigan, 2016; Vance, 2004

whole-class instrumental lessons, or a school's class music lessons, or ensemble teaching. Moreover, if individual lessons are the only musical experience the student with dyslexia has, this is a socially *exclusive* practice. We must also bear in mind that instrumental teachers can experience constraints in the lesson formats they can offer (see Chapter 1). So, differentiation is key, but it is important to note that many of the pedagogical ideas mentioned in this chapter can benefit non-dyslexic learners as well.

Task duration and learner fatigue

Another consideration relates to visual disruption, the higher level of concentration required of music learners with dyslexia as a result, and fatigue. Lesson planning might involve teaching sessions, or at least continuous activities within them of a shorter duration. Scheduling short breaks may also be helpful.

Should teachers select musical genres where notation
is less dominant or absent?

Learners with dyslexia will *in different ways* grapple with music-reading. The writers Nelson and Hourigan (2016) have suggested that instrumental teachers select musical genres for them where notation is less dominant or even absent (e.g., some jazz, popular music, traditional music, etc. relying instead on playing by ear). However, this may limit the capability of learners to participate in notation-based genres in future. Again, this is socially exclusive thinking. It has implications for the student's long-term musical engagement. There is also the flawed assumption that the instrumental learner will automatically be interested in, and thus motivated by, the afore-mentioned musical genres. That simply might not be the case. So, the long-term goals and aspirations of students should be an important consideration in shaping the learning process, in planning the repertoire to be studied and in gauging the significance of music-reading skills and knowledge.

It is also prudent to consider that, if any learner finds an aspect of their music troublesome (in this case, music reading), this need not mean it should be avoided altogether. It is natural to wish to take the easiest path, and we all do that sometimes, even subconsciously.

However, perhaps this is a matter of, *on one side*, avoidance of surmounting an obstacle and, *on the other*, addressing learner weaknesses thus using them to focus and drive learning. Good instrumental teachers whose work is sharply focussed on the formative will favour of the latter.

Delaying music reading and aural approaches first: It has become *sine qua non* in music teaching that sound goes before symbol. This gives primacy to the desired sounds being internalised (such that the learner can hear them in his or her mind) ahead of acquiring knowledge of the corresponding symbol on his or her score. This applies to instrumentalists with dyslexia too. This reasoning has led to innovative pedagogical approaches in music education such as involving playing by ear in response to audio recordings without scores,[12] and even some of the longstanding ones that place a strong emphasis on listening and modelling (such as the Suzuki method). Some of these have reported faster aural skill development in music learners due to the immersive listening involved.[13] Often, the reverse, that is, starting with the music symbol, is seen as placing the cart before the horse.

Since notation can serve as an obstacle for instrumental learners with dyslexia, some writers[14] recommend learning by ear before proceeding with score reading. It has also been suggested that the Suzuki approach, which initially concentrates on focussed listening with the teacher modelling, has a part to play for people with dyslexia. This entails the learner initially watching, for example, hand and arm movements, and observing technique, *but significantly without notation*. We do need to be mindful of potential memory deficits in learners with dyslexia and possible challenges with their fine motor skills. Certainly, listening, modelling and repetition away from the notation for embedding aural and technical skills may take on special significance for beginner instrumentalists with dyslexia,[15] or even for more developed players when learning a new piece.[16]

---

12 e.g., Lucy Green's informal learning pedagogy, see Green, 2008; also see Batt-Rawden & Denora, 2005; Hallam, Creech & McQueen, 2015, 2016; Lebler, 2008; Narita, 2015
13 e.g., Baker, 2013; Baker & Green, 2013   14 e.g., Macmillan, 2008   15 Macmillan, 2008
16 Backhouse, 2001; Ganschow, 1994

However, this might be seen as a complementary strategy rather than a long-term replacement pedagogy if learners wish to pursue musical interests that involve reading.

Teaching case study – Michael and Elias

Elias (pseudonym) is an intelligent, upbeat 14-year-old. He is an intermediate trumpet player (B♭ trumpet). His weekly lessons take place at his UK secondary (high) school. Elias has dyslexia of which his teacher Michael (pseudonym) is aware. They have found that a balance of learning by ear, particularly in the earliest stages of approaching pieces, and stave notation reading, proves successful. In previous discussions, Elias has mentioned how notation is essential for his desire of a place in the county youth orchestra. He also wishes to pursue the higher ABRSM (Associated Board of the Royal Schools of Music) instrumental grade examinations.

Week 1

Michael (teacher): Let's start learning the first phrases of a new grade piece, but without your music. It's good for your aural skills. I'll play the first phrase then I'd like you to copy me.

Elias (pupil): Okay.

Michael: Just to stretch you a bit more, try not to look at me. I want you to use your ears. Turn away slightly. I'll tell you that the key is F major and the starting note is a C on the ledger line below the treble stave. So, start with no valves pushed down. There is one accidental, so a note that doesn't fit into the scale of F major.

Michael plays the phrase as Elias listens. Elias subsequently attempts to repeat it. He does this several times. As he does, the lesson progresses with Michael pointing out any errors in Elias's pitch and rhythm. Michael does this by performing Elias's incorrect versions and the correct one for comparison and discussion. The focus is security of pitch and rhythm at this point and there is no discussion of the interpretation and dynamics, etc.

Michael: Let's think about the upward interval at the start. The second note you played was a G, so your first two notes were C then G. I'll play that and then how those should sound. Can you tell me the difference?

Michael plays an upward perfect fifth (C–G), then a perfect fourth (C–F).

Michael: What did you notice?

Elias: My second note was too high. Maybe I need to try an F instead. That would explain why I got a bit lost [with the melody] before getting back on track.

Michael: Excellent. You've got good ears. Try an F then and let's see if you're right.

Elias makes another attempt, and Michael confirms it is correct. The lesson continues in this way, with Michael playing, then Elias, with Michael also demonstrating correct then incorrect ingredients for discussion. Elias's performances of the first phrase gradually become far more secure. However, Michael turns his attention to perfecting the rhythm. He takes his left hand off his trumpet and slaps his thigh gently as he plays to indicate the pulse, again also giving demonstrations of where Elias had gone awry for analysis. When Elias plays his attempts, Michael claps the pulse. By the end of this segment of the lesson, lasting about 20 minutes, Elias has achieved the first three phrases of his new piece. They then turn to a piece they have been working on from notation. However, before they do, Michael makes a recording of the first three phrases on an audio recorder so that this can be used during home practice. Elias has brought this to the lesson.

Week 2

Michael: How did everything go with practising the new piece at home?

Elias: Good. The recording helped.

Michael: That sounds great.

Elias: I'm still stuck a bit with the last phrase.

Michael: Okay, we'll sort that out. Let's use the sheet music
    this time.

*Michael listens as Elias plays the piece. However, there is an error
with a rhythm in the third phrase. Elias is playing a minim (half
note) rather than a crotchet (quarter note).*

Michael: Okay, the pitch and rhythm of most of it is good. Well
    done. There's just a small slip here.

Michael points at the relevant notes on the score.

Michael: I'd like you to clap a steady pulse. I'm going to play it how
    you did, then the correct way and, a bit like last time, tell me the
    difference.
Elias: Do I start clapping first.
Michael: That's right. Give me four beats in and I'll start at the
    beginning of the phrase.

*They begin. Michael points with his left hand as he plays.
He performs the phrase twice, first in the incorrect then
the correct manner.*

Michael: Did you spot the difference?
Elias: Yes. I played the note there for too long. It should have been
    one beat not two.
Michael: Exactly. Can you point to the symbol for a crotchet,
    or one beat, and then show me a minim, two, somewhere else
    on the score? How do they look different?

*Commentary: A 'sound before symbol' approach has been taken
here, with a dedicated segment of the first lesson, to cement
the kinaesthetic capabilities and procedural memories needed
to perform the piece effectively away from notation initially. This
simultaneously develops aural skills. However, this was clearly just
a starting point, or supplementary tactic, for notation reading since
a playful 'spot the difference' approach was subsequently taken*

forward in the next lesson using the score. This was motivational for Elias as he is underway with his piece before being confronted with score reading, which he finds arduous due to his dyslexia.

Using audio recordings

The literature on music pedagogy also highlights the use of audio recordings to supplement working from a score[17] (also see the case study, above). Professional musicians with dyslexia researched by Nelson and Hourigan (2016) noted the importance of this in their long-term success. Technologies have made this much easier in instrumental lessons in recent years. The learner's smartphone, for example, can record his or her teacher performing sections of pieces or, indeed, complete pieces, which can be taken home for practice. Recordings can also be made of the student within lessons for comparison with a teacher's performance i.e., for reflection and identification of what is correct and incorrect. Resultant discussions build critical listening and aural perception skills into instrumental lessons.

Multisensory approaches

Multisensory approaches, that is, those where learners are taught visually, aurally and kinaesthetically, may be helpful for instrumental pupils with dyslexia. For example, they may have issues with the abstract concepts of higher and lower pitch. Accordingly, Heikkila and Knight (2012) offer an example of the teacher pointing and singing from music notation while children with dyslexia follow the melodic contour with their hands in the air. In another example, these authors explain a musical game whereby children sing a three-note ostinato and gently tap their head, arm and lap in-keeping with the pitches. Oglethorpe (2008b) advocates a large stave on the floor created with masking tape for a whole-body learning experience. She remarks that learners can stand on this and be asked to jump to different notes, for example, 'Jump to the E in a space', or they can be asked to spell out specified words in letter names (e.g., 'egg'

---

17 Nelson & Hourigan, 2016; Vance, 2004

or 'face' etc.). Colour can also be utilised in various ways, and this is discussed later in this chapter.

Lisa Carlin[18] considers teaching instrumentalists with dyslexia a matter of using a multisensory 'package' that can be tweaked for individuals. This is due to the wide continuum of dyslexia circumstances.[19] There is scope for teachers to be creative. Equally though, those with SpLDs may be quickly overloaded. This needs to be borne in mind when approaching rhythm, for instance. Asking a pupil to watch his or her teacher, coordinate tapping his or her foot in time, count the beat aloud and clap a rhythm may be a step too far. Particularly so if he or she has, for example, dyspraxia or comorbid motor issues as well. It might be more sensible to simplify, for example, with the teacher establishing a steady pulse by tapping his or her foot, and the teacher and pupil clapping the rhythm together in unison.

Focussing on musical constituents separately, breaking tasks down and repetition

It might also be helpful to break learning into its separable components initially. This can happen in various ways: for instance, the pitches of a melody can be played before adding the rhythmic content, or vice versa, or the fingering can be practised before playing the notes, or small chunks of material (rhythmic, melodic) can be addressed separately, or work can be done on component lines in a polyphonic texture first, etc. Brass and woodwind players might benefit, for example, from rehearsing the rhythm by pressing their valves or keys without the added complication of producing sound.[20] Overloading the student with the expectation that, at the first attempt, he or she can achieve, or even sight-read the pitch, rhythm, correct tempo and tempo changes, dynamics, phrasing, other performance directions, or even a complex texture, etc. may be disheartening. It may be helpful instead to think in terms of a 'layers and layering' approach *where possible* (adding one ingredient at a time) to engender competence and confidence in

---

18 online discussion on 10 July 2025   19 also see Carlin, 2015   20 Oglethorpe, 2002

the learner, but more gradually than for others, with repetitions and reinforcement. Research has indicated that professional musicians with dyslexia have learned in this manner.[21] Musical ingredients that might be considered separately within a layering strategy, and not implying hierarchical order, might include:

- Pitches (including due diligence to any key signature)
- Rhythms
- Any repeated melodic or rhythmic structures (e.g., motifs, ostinati, etc.)
- Bars and metre, and their impact on emphases
- Component lines in polyphonic textures
- Dynamics
- Symbolic performance directions (accent signs, staccato dots, etc.)
- Textual performance directions (written instructions on the score)
- Tempi and tempo changes

Teaching case study – Shreya and Adam

Shreya teaches Adam the flute. He is 10 years old and visits Shreya's home with his mother for lessons. These weekly sessions take place in Shreya's kitchen and Adam's mother waits in her living room. Adam has been having the lessons for just over two years. He has dyslexia with mild, comorbid Autism Spectrum Disorder (ASD). He receives additional support at his primary (elementary) school with reading and writing. Adam is clearly a determined child who, despite struggling with music reading, is admirably persistent.

Shreya and Adam are working on one of his ABRSM Grade 3 examination pieces together. They are in a second week of exploring it. She opens Adam's music book, which is on the music stand, and begins.

---

21 Nelson & Hourigan, 2016

Shreya (teacher): It's a fast piece, right, in a joyful mood. Play the rhythm in a jaunty way, like you're happy and mischievous. Leaving tiny gaps between the notes and lean on the first note of each four in those figures. Do you see the accent signs? Don't forget the crescendo towards the highest note in this phrase too, before getting quieter as you descend again. Keep the rhythm going by counting in your head but, as you get to the end, notice there is a slight rallentando.

Adam remains silent. He does not question what he is being asked to do. He attempts the piece.

Shreya: Stop. You got the rhythm wrong there. It's longer like this, and the third note has a sharp. Do you understand what I mean?
Adam (pupil): Yes.

Shreya points at the parts of the score where Adam made the mistakes as part of her explanation. She now plays a correct rendition of the phrase. Adam makes another attempt.

Shreya: No. That's not right either. You got the accidental right, but there were no dynamics. What about the crescendo and diminuendo? Let's review what needs to go into this. You need to count more carefully, as the rhythm still wasn't quite right. Put in the accents and accidental sharp, but the dynamics and style are also very important.
Adam: Sorry.
Shreya: You do understand what I want you to do, don't you?
Adam: Yes.
Shreya: Good.

Adam has another failed attempt. He begins to look frustrated.

What went wrong? *Adam's dyslexia likely meant that he was overloaded by too many musical ingredients at once. He was being asked to process the pitches, rhythm, articulation, dynamics,* *tempo change and the emotional aspects of the performance. Shreya had not understood this was an issue for Adam. She had not appreciated that he needed to approach pieces with a more measured approach whereby the various ingredients were progressively introduced and built up. She had also not realised that her instructions were very long and convoluted for a child with comorbid ASD. He also perhaps struggled to comprehend the metaphorical and emotional aspects of her language use (see Chapter 3). Shreya attempted to ascertain whether Adam had understood her requirements for the performance, but her approach was ineffective as she simply accepted his 'Yes' responses on this, rather than finding a way to test his understanding. Adam may have misunderstood, or not understood at all, but was too embarrassed to be candid. It is easy to see why Adam rapidly became disheartened.*

Interim summary

Some considerations for the instrumental teacher:

- *Consider* the length of activities within lessons, particularly the duration of continuous ones without breaks. Add breaks. This might be part of the teacher's routine, informal oversight of lessons but could be written into lesson planning too. Learners with dyslexia can become fatigued more rapidly and their concentration may wain.
- *Consult* students on their long-term aims in relation to participation in musical genres and performing contexts to understand how important notation reading will be to them.
- *Employ* a sound-before-symbol stance with beginners, if helpful, that places the internalisation of sounds ahead of music reading. This might also apply to more advanced pupils with dyslexia when they address new repertoire.
- *Use* recording devices to support the learning process. However, do so prudently. As an example, recordings of score elements might be referenced in home practice, so that the student can respond by ear in tandem with reading notation.

However, be wary that audio might be used to circumvent learning to read.

- *Create* a range of adaptable multisensory activities to engage the visual, aural and kinaesthetic senses. Ponder whole-body experiences or those that engage learners with dyslexia in establishing musical concepts away from their instrument in the first instance.
- *Distinguish* score ingredients that can be addressed separately and in a progressively layered approach. For instance, perhaps the pitches of a melodic line might be addressed separately from the rhythm before putting these together. Gradually introduce and combine these ingredients, progressively adding complexity, so as not to overload the learner.

Music reading

Music notation, visual disruption and fatigue

Stave notation is dense with abstract signs and symbols. *For pitch*, for example, these include stave and ledger lines (and the position of noteheads on them), key signatures, note stems (and their direction), etc. *For metre, rhythm and emphasis*, key information comes from time signatures, bar lines, notehead styles, note flags and beaming (indicating rhythm and rhythmic structures), etc. There are also *interpretive symbols* such as phrase marks, accents, staccato dots, etc. Then there are *textual directions* either for overall tempi and performance style, such as 'Allegro con brio' (fast with vigour), or for finer details within the score, e.g., 'con sordini' (with a mute), 'rallentando' (gradually slow down) or 'dolce' (sweetly), etc. Often, the latter are Italian terms, but they may also be in other languages too depending on the repertoire being studied. When we start to categorise the various meanings within music's signs and symbols in this way (i.e., in terms of pitch, metre, rhythm, emphasis, interpretation, textual instructions), as well as contemplating the vast permutations of some of them, it becomes apparent that a fluent music reader might easily overlook the complexity of stave notation for learners with dyslexia.

Sheila Oglethorpe (2002) remarks that instrumental learners with dyslexia may experience visual disruption when reading music. This reportedly may entail the parallel lines of scores (the stave lines) appearing to move. She also suggests that learners may struggle to focus on a single point and/or have poor visual tracking. When experienced music readers perform from sheet music, they typically read ahead (often bars ahead of their current point, scanning back and forth with their eyes), and they can scan across stave systems (going from the end of one to the start of the next below on a page, or from the bottom of one page to the top of another). Visual tracking is an important aspect of reading stave notation and fluent sight-reading. However, this may be far more challenging for some learners with dyslexia. Later in this chapter we look at how the use of colour on scores might help. Moreover, music reading may quickly lead to visual fatigue due to the stresses caused by visual tracking issues. Whilst repetition is undoubtedly important for advancing technical skills and for achieving sound performances in any instrumentalist, it may be imperative for these learners to take regular breaks.

Understanding the student's approach

As mentioned in Chapter 1, effective instrumental teachers are explorers in the sense that they want to understand fully their students' thought processes as an ongoing endeavour. This applies to instrumental teachers working with any student. Without understanding our pupils' reasoning in relation to what they are learning, their approaches and strategies, it is more difficult to put in place corrective measures or, indeed, to confirm they are right. So questioning is vital in instrumental teaching to draw out this information, for example, "How did you work that rhythm out?", or "What was your strategy for finding the pitches?", etc. 'How', 'what' and 'why' questions elicit such information.

When students experience difficulties with music reading due to SEND, it is natural that they might find ingenious means to overcome them, sometimes sidestepping a better way. It might even be that, in some cases, they desire to hide inadequate understanding due to low self-esteem or embarrassment (see Chapter 1). There are examples in the literature suggesting music learners with dyslexia can use flawed, compensatory strategies to disguise their problems.[22] Unfortunately, those tactics may lead them down a blind alley. Consider a beginner instrumentalist with dyslexia, for example, ascertaining the pitches and melodic contour by focussing on the tops of the note stems. That might work so far, for example, until pitches go above the middle line of the treble stave in a new piece (and thus switch direction), or when a new score has stems of a different length. Another beginner might equate the duration of notes to their horizontal spacing, understanding crotchets (quarter note) as double the duration of quavers (eighth note) because the latter are closer together (half the horizontal distance) on their current score. If the student has not understood the symbolic implications of noteheads, note-flags and beaming, he or she will eventually run into problems. His or her approach might work until a more complicated score has less even or obvious spacing. Evidently then, music teachers require detailed knowledge of how their students are 'going about it' to prevent misunderstandings and support students with better strategies to drive progression.

Teaching case study – Grace and Abisai

Abisai is a beginner violinist. He has had one-to-one lessons for a term at his UK secondary school. Abisai is in Year 7 and is 11 years old. His teacher, Grace, started him with simple exercises of notated rhythms on single pitches bowed on open strings in semibreves (whole notes), minims (half notes) and crotchets (quarter notes). The learning progressed rapidly. Abisai is now attempting a piece that begins by leaping upwards from an E to a B:

---

22 see e.g., Oglethorpe, 2002; Tunmer & Greaney, 2010

Abisai starts his piece with his finger correctly positioned on the D string to produce an E. However, he unconfidently plays a lower second note on his G string, a C, with poor intonation. Grace is surprised by this.

Grace (teacher): Abisai, the second note is higher. I'll play it for you to copy. Listen carefully and watch.

Grace plays the ascending E (D string) to B (A string) interval as Abisai watches. He copies this correctly, yet in another place in the piece makes the same mistake as before.

Grace: How are you working out the pitches, Abisai?
Abisai (pupil): You find the end of the lines. That tells you how high or low to play. Then you need to decide on the right string and finger position.
Grace: Ah, I see what's happening. You're looking at the top of the note stems and should be looking at the note heads.

What went wrong? *Abisai was under the impression that the top of note stems indicated the pitches. Feasibly this misconceived strategy had gone unnoticed by Grace while he was playing pieces, or passages of pieces, where the notes had never extended onto and above the middle line of the treble stave. At that point, the note stems had begun to point downwards sometimes. Now, Abisai was faced with a confusing situation with some stems pointing upwards and some downwards. In this instance (i.e., in the music example above), Abisai had perhaps remembered the first note (E) from a previous lesson, so played it correctly. This was reinforced when Grace demonstrated. However, the stem of the second note (now pointing downwards) was slightly below the level of the first notehead (that of the E) seemingly directing Abisai to play a lower pitch (C). When Grace played the correct pitches, he simply watched and copied, but this had not cleared up his misunderstanding about the notation. Accordingly, he continued to make the mistake elsewhere in his piece.*

Score enlargements

Some literature proposes that enlarging scores can be advantageous for music learners with dyslexia.[23] The scale of enlargements requires careful consideration however, since there are reasonable limits to physical size and manageability. This also needs to be planned carefully with pupil consultation and close monitoring regarding whether it helps.

Note names

If too much emphasis is placed on identifying letter names in the early stages, this might be frustrating and, ultimately, detrimental for some learners with dyslexia. Piano scores, for instance, offer a potentially bewildering gamut of different letter names for the ten lines and eight spaces of the bass and treble staves (not yet factoring in ledger lines), and multiple notes with the same name at different pitches.

Conceivably of more consequence then, particularly in the earliest stages, are listening and responding to teacher modelling – the aforesaid sound before symbol approach – and concentrating on the visible intervals and melodic contour on the score rather than the note names themselves.[24] Here too is another rationale for making audio recordings available since instrumentalists with dyslexia may have short-term memory problems. When a piece, or parts of it, have consequently been learned kinaesthetically (at which point the player's fingers are on 'autopilot', the piece memorised, and the sounds internalised), note-name recognition might become a more pressing endeavour. This might be particularly so for beginner instrumentalists. Having made these remarks though, readers should heed the significant caveats in the passages above (see 'Delaying music reading' and 'Using audio recordings'). There is likely a balance to be struck, hence the examples of a multisensory approach to learning letter names mentioned earlier. This is because the eventual aim will be for the learner to read fluently rather than relying principally on playing by ear coupled

---

23 Heikkila & Knight, 2012; Hubicki, 2001; Oglethorpe, 2002 24 Oglethorpe, 2002b

with only a partial or sketchy understanding of the scores he or she encounters.

Geometry and spatial awareness: Up, down, left, right

Pianists with dyslexia may experience geometrical and spatial awareness issues when reading music. With stave notation, it is *up* for higher pitches (along with treble stave being above its bass counterpart), which may be seemingly incongruous for learners with dyslexia as the higher pitches of the keyboard are *to the right*. There are two planes: *vertically up and down* on the score, versus *left to right* on the keyboard itself. Any confusion may be coupled with the pianist's right hand being off to the right (for higher notes, treble stave) relative to the left (for lower notes, bass), i.e., rather than above the left hand in line with the visual representation of the score. To illustrate the problems that can occur, Oglethorpe (2002) provides an anecdote of an 8-year-old who was asked to write a higher note than one she had written. The child did this by writing on the right-hand edge of the paper.

Short-term teaching strategies that have been recommended involve turning the score on its side (rotating clockwise by 90 degrees), so that pitch on the score matches the geometry of the piano keyboard. The suggestion is that this should be done in tandem with writing all the bass clef stems downwards (which will subsequently be to the left) and all the treble clef ones upwards (subsequently to the right).[25] A sheet music book could be held open at by the piano teacher so it does not close, or, alternatively, its pages might be printed out and pasted onto a large piece of card to avoid the score flopping over. There are provisos in this author's view: firstly, confirmation is required that this is, indeed, the student's issue; secondly, the aforesaid solution is reported as effective by an experienced teacher of pianists with dyslexia and, while it may be so, this needs confirmation through research and other music educators' accounts; and, thirdly, this should be seen as a short-term solution since the learner must eventually cope with the normal orientation of music notation.

---

25 Oglethorpe, 2002

Note stem direction: Note stems do appear to cause considerable confusion for instrumentalists with dyslexia. Research seems to indicate that having all the stems in the same direction improves music reading performance.[26] The inverted stem of higher notes might seem to pull them lower psychologically, or conversely, the upright stems of lower ones upwards. Adjusting scores so that all the stems are in the same direction can be achieved with correction fluid and writing in alternative stems, or by using digital music engraving software. However, there are some important points for the instrumental teacher to consider: *firstly*, the student may be incorrectly interpreting the pitches of notes by looking at the tops of the stems (as in the case study, 'Grace and Abisai', above, and that should be monitored); *secondly*, the length of stems may be different within new scores due to typesetting practices; and, *thirdly*, the goal, ultimately, might be for the learner to cope with typical notation. Adjusting the direction of note stems may be a suitable short-term strategy, or help when addressing new pieces, but the instrumental teacher and his or her pupil might well decide that it is only that.

Colour and learning materials

Utilising colour may be a helpful tactic. The pedagogical literature repeatedly suggests various ways in which it might be used, including:

- changing the colour of paper on which stave notation is printed (e.g., to a pastel colour)
- using sheets of tinted acetate placed over the score
- wearing tinted glasses
- highlighting or colour-coding score elements (e.g., with highlighter pens)

The first suggestion, above, is to print notation on suitably coloured paper, often a pastel shade, to avoid glare.[27] It is thought this

---

26 e.g., Flach, Timmermans & Korpershoek, 2016
27 Heikkila & Knight, 2012; O'Brien, 2004; Oglethorpe, 2002

mitigates against eye function problems. Some researchers and writers have argued there is a lack of evidence for this.[28] The second and third are either to place a sheet of tinted acetate over the score or wear tinted glasses.[29] Again, this is to reduce glare and aid the instrumental student's concentration. It would be important to be conscious of any distracting reflections either in the acetate sheet or glasses resulting from the lighting in one's teaching room. Again, these ideas require confirmation as effective, perhaps by testing them in specific teaching situations with individual students.

The fourth idea is to use colour for score elements, which might include highlighting to indicate, for example:

- different pitches
- repeated motifs and other melodic structures within a piece
- the position of rests relative to played notes in polyphonic texture (e.g., with vertical bands of colour blocked through the treble and bass staves on individual beats in a piano score)[30]
- new concepts and skills that are being introduced, e.g., the pupils' first attempt at articulation symbols (*staccato*, *legato*)[31]
- repeat signs with an arrow to where they lead (for better visual tracking)
- the starting bar after a page turn (as above)

Much can be done with coloured highlighter pens. The intention is to support the instrumental learner in identifying structures and breaking them down into digestible chunks, including repetitions thereof, and to assist in visual tracking in performance and sight-reading. Figure 1 (reproduced in greyscale and annotated) illustrates coloured noteheads produced with Steinberg's Dorico 4 music engraving software:

---

28 see Reifinger, 2019   **29** Oglethorpe, 2002   **30** Oglethorpe, 2002   **31** Vance, 2004

Figure 1. W. A. Mozart, Rondo from Horn Concerto No. 4 in E♭ major, K495 with coloured noteheads

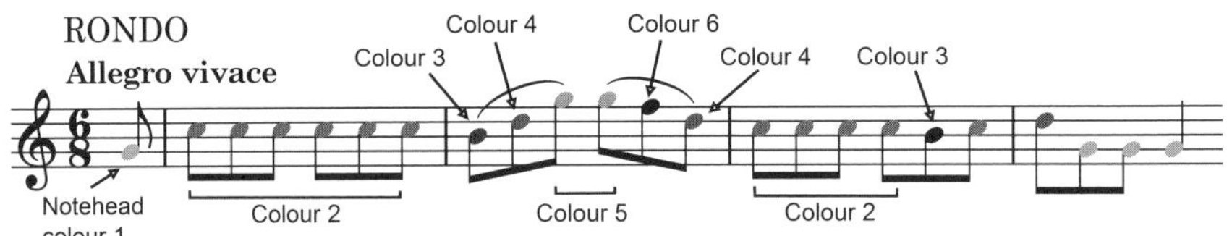

The position of rests in one part against played notes in the other can be indicated by vertical blocks of colour across the two score systems.[32] Some expert teachers[33] have also suggested writing in notes instead of rests, but bracketing them as not to be played, but this seems contrary to the score decluttering mentioned below.

When using colour on scores however, we must be cognisant that its effectiveness depends on what is optimal for individual students. We should neither suppose that colouring is a universally effective teaching practice underpinned by research, just because expert teachers say so, nor assume that using it is automatically helpful.

In their research project, Flach, Timmermans and Korpershoek (2016) asked children to identify notes from short, printed music examples. The children were given various examples that were coloured and non-coloured, had either all the stems up, or, alternatively, down, and where the score was regular sized or enlarged. Although the children they tested with dyslexia made more errors, this was reduced by enlargements and by writing all the note stems in the same direction. However, they found the use of coloured stave lines counterproductive.

Decluttering scores

Instrumental teachers might wish to make an assessment about what on the printed score is being studied at any given time (also see 'Focussing on musical constituents separately' above). Instinctively in my experience, instrumental teachers tend to work with their

---

32 Oglethorpe, 2002   **33** e.g., Oglethorpe, 2002

students in layers of complexity in relation to scores. They do so in a progressive manner, by starting with simple ideas, skills and understandings before gradually proceeding to more complicated ones, particularly so with beginners. For instance, when a lesson introduces a piece with new pitches that the beginner student has not seen before, it is unlikely that equal attention will be paid to the dynamics, articulation, finer textual performance directions or phrasing, etc. (at least initially). Those will be added later. The spotlight will be on getting the pitches and rhythm correct. Yet, there is much information on the score that *at that moment* is superfluous and maybe distracting or even confusing for the instrumentalist with dyslexia. Decluttering scores might, therefore, be helpful. This can be done either by removing details with correction fluid (with multiple photocopies of out-of-copyright material so these can be reintroduced) or by using music engraving software (such as Dorico, MuseScore or Sibelius). Oglethorpe (2002) also suggests that 'agreed signs' can be put in place on reintroduction to show, for example, where a phrase ends.

Teaching case study – Marta and Oliver

Marta is a piano teacher. Her pupil, Oliver, has dyslexia. He finds reading stave notation demanding at times but, nevertheless, possible. They have agreed that this is a key pursuit given Oliver's aims, not least to take his GCSE (General Certificate of Secondary Education) secondary school music examination. He is in Year 9 and is 14 years old. Oliver's weekly individual lessons take place during the school day in a small practice room.

Marta has made two photo-enlargements of a new piece for Oliver to play. This is 'L'Arabesque' from 25 Études faciles et progressives *Op. 100 No. 2 by Friedrich Burgmüller. On the first version, Marta has removed the dynamics, the articulation (staccato dots), phrase marks, the expression text (e.g.,* leggiero*), the composer's name and his dates. She has left the main tempo 'Allegro scherzando' at the start of the first system. This has been done with correction fluid. The second version is the same, but with the dynamics reintroduced. The piece begins with repeated*

*chords in crotchets (quarter notes) in the left hand, which, after
two bars, are joined by melodic patterns in semi-quaver groups
and quavers (sixteenth and eighth notes) in the right.*

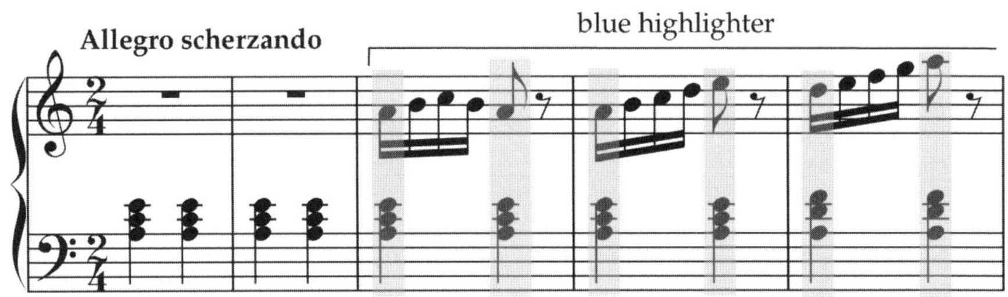

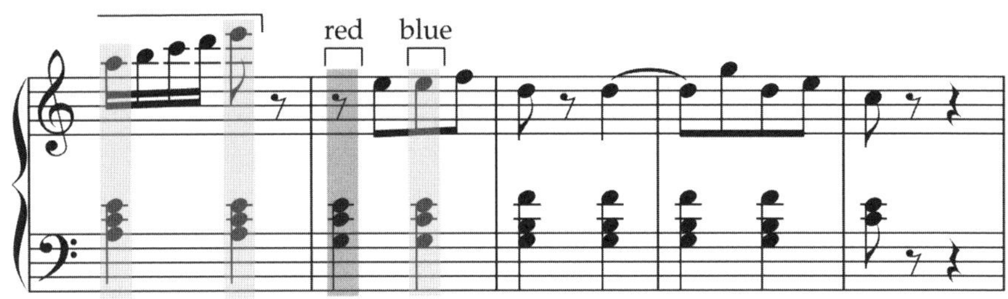

Marta (teacher): It's a new piece so I've removed all the
distractions. We can look at how to add style and interpretation
later. Let's start hands separately. Play the first six bars of the
left-hand part.

*After working on the piece hands separately, first with the left
hand then right, they begin to discuss how the two fit together
rhythmically. Marta is keen to involve Oliver in marking this new
knowledge onto his score, so she produces a blue highlighter pen.*

Marta: Oliver, point at the score and show me the first time the
left- and right-hand parts happen at the same time.
Oliver: It's here.
Marta: Good. Yes, that's right. There's a two-bar introduction in
the left-hand in crotchet chords. The right hand joins in at the
start of the third bar. That's where both hands happen at the
same time. Draw a vertical line through all the notes [there]
that happen at the same time.

They continue to work through the score discussing coinciding left- and right-hand notes, marking them as they go. These mostly occur on the beat. In bar 7 however (see the music example above), there is a quaver rest (eighth note rest) at the start of the bar in the right hand. It is where the left-hand chord on the first beat of that bar corresponds to a quaver (eighth note) rest in the right hand. Marta asks Oliver to mark this with a red highlighter pen.

Commentary: Marta stripped back the score as much as viable to remove information that could be addressed later, but she also had a strategy to reinstate it (e.g., the articulation then the dynamics, etc.). She involved Oliver in marking his score, which was a good way to appraise his understanding.

Navigating systems and repeats

Colour and arrows might be exploited for navigating jumps between systems, repeat signs and first- and second-time bars. Sheila Oglethorpe (2002) offers some interesting recommendations: Scores can be reformatted when their systems are close together, which she reports as advantageous. These can be made further apart on non-copyright material by photocopying, cutting them out with scissors and pasting them onto large sheets of card. Alternatively, engraving software can ensure adequate system spacing. Oglethorpe also recommends a long, coloured line made with a highlighter pen between the two staves of each piano system that, at its right-hand end then becomes a new colour for the next system down, etc. (see Figure 2 below). This aids the learner in knowing where to jump next. A stipulation to this is that too many coloured elements (i.e., for various aspects of scores) may start to cause confusion.

Figure 2. Sheila Oglethorpe's (2002) aid to navigating systems applied to Johann Sebastian Bach, Prelude in C major, BWV 846

Some considerations for the instrumental teacher
(interim summary):

- *Appreciate* the complexity of neurodiversity with dyslexia representing a vast catalogue of widely varying conditions, possible comorbidities and experiences. Thus, the effectiveness of any strategy rests on the individual learner's needs. It is important to innovate, try ideas, discuss their usefulness with learners and constantly monitor.
- *Seek* to understand the learner's score-reading strategies with 'how', 'what' and 'why' reflective questioning. This assumes they are verbal, without comorbid ASD or intellectual disabilities significantly impacting communication. Never take for granted that learners have understood ideas and concepts, or that their strategy matches yours.
- *Enlarge* scores, but only if it is agreed this is helpful.
- *Model* and involve the learner in aural learning. Trial addressing the material in this way first with beginners, then address the note names, that is, if music reading is a viable or important enterprise.

- *Try* writing all the note stems in the same direction (use engraving software, or correction fluid), but as a short-term strategy only.
- *Discuss* with the learner whether tinted glasses, paper, or acetate help, including how this relates to their reading of text.
- *Experiment* by using colour to highlight elements on scores, so that the learner can identify and break down structures (including any repeated ones).
- *Declutter* scores and gradually re-introduce their symbolic and textual complexity. Consider what needs to be learned at any given time.
- *Use* vertical blocks of colour across the staves of e.g., piano scores or duets, to show the position of notes played against rests.
- *Support* visual tracking by spacing systems and staves adequately. Perhaps utilise arrows or colour strategies to guide the learner in his or her navigation.
- *Balance* the urge to add further elements to scores with the present capabilities of the learner. In adding seemingly helpful colour, or arrows, or bespoke signs, etc. be cautious not to overload him or her.

Reflective questions

- What are the benefits of learning an instrument for people with dyslexia?
- What challenges does stave music notation present?
- How might multisensory learning be formed for instrumentalists with dyslexia?
- In what ways might colour be used to support music reading?

Suggested further reading

Backhouse, G. (2001). A pianist's story. In T. R. Miles, & J. Westcombe (Eds.), *Music and dyslexia: Opening new doors* (Ch. 19). Whurr.

Daunt, S. (2012). *Music, other performing arts and dyslexia*. British Dyslexia Association.

Ganschow, L., Lloyd-Jones, J., & Miles, T. R. (1994). Dyslexia and musical notation. *Annals of Dyslexia, 44*, 185–202.

Heikkila, E., & Knight, A. (2012). Inclusive music teaching strategies for elementary-age children with developmental dyslexia. *Music Educators Journal, 99*(1), 54–59.

Honeybourne, V. (2018). *The neurodiverse classroom: A teacher's guide to individual learning needs and how to meet them.* Jessica Kingsley.

Miles, T., Westcombe, J., & Ditchfield, D. (Eds.). (2008). *Music and dyslexia: A positive approach.* John Wiley and Sons.

Nelson, K. P., & Hourigan, R. M. (2016). A comparative case study of learning strategies and recommendations of five professional musicians with dyslexia. *Update: Applications of Research in Music Education, 35*(1), 54–65.

O'Brien, V. K. (2004). Adapting music instruction for students with dyslexia. *Music Educators Journal, 90*(5), 27–31.

Oglethorpe, S. M. (2002). *Instrumental music for dyslexics: A teaching handbook* (2nd ed.). Whurr.

Oglethorpe, S. M. (2008a). Can music lessons help the dyslexic learner? In T. Miles, J. Westcombe, & D. Ditchfield (Eds.), *Music and dyslexia: A positive approach* (pp. 57–67). John Wiley and Sons.

Oglethorpe, S. M. (2008b). Sight-reading. In T. Miles, J. Westcombe, & D. Ditchfield (Eds.), *Music and dyslexia: A positive approach* (pp. 82–91). John Wiley and Sons.

Overy, K. (2000). Dyslexia, temporal processing and music: The potential of music as an early learning aid for dyslexic children. *Psychology of Music, 28*(2), 218–229.

Reifinger, J. L. (2019). Dyslexia in the music classroom: A review of literature. *Update: Applications of Research in Music Education, 38*(1), 9–17.

Snowling, M. (1997). *Dyslexia: A cognitive developmental perspective.* Blackwell.

Tunmer, W., & Greaney, K. (2010). Defining dyslexia. *Journal of Learning Disabilities, 43*(3), 229–243.

Vance, K. O. (2004). Adapting music instruction for students with dyslexia. *Music Educators Journal, 90*(5), 2–72.

3

Autism Spectrum Disorder

What is Autism Spectrum Disorder (ASD)?

Autism Spectrum Disorder (ASD), known informally as 'autism', is a condition affecting social interaction, cognition and communication, sometimes in tandem with restricted and repetitive behaviours (e.g., strong interests in specific topics, repetitive body movements and sensory sensitivities).[1] It is a lifelong condition shaping a person's interactions and thus development. The UK's National Health Service points out that it '…is not a medical condition with treatments or a "cure"', or a disease, but, rather, means that a person will need certain types and levels of support.[2] It might also be prudent to note that some dislike the term '*dis*-order' (as discussed in Chapter 1) in favour of understanding autism as a neurodiversity 'difference'.

ASD equates to a vast spectrum of unique circumstances, so nothing can be assumed regarding music learners. It ranges, e.g., from people who function very independently in society who do not immediately appear autistic, i.e., with average or above average intelligence, to those who have major learning disabilities and communication issues who will need considerable support with daily life. The American Psychiatric Association (2013) has stratified ASD into three severity levels: Level 1, i.e., 'requiring support', Level 2, 'requiring substantial support', and Level 3, 'requiring very substantial support'. ASD has been found to have substantial comorbidity with other neurodevelopmental conditions too, including e.g., dyslexia (see Chapter 2).[3] It can also occur with e.g., Attention Deficit Hyperactivity Disorder (ADHD),[4] epilepsy, anxiety, depression, etc. making for a plethora of conceivable personal circumstances.

---

1 American Psychiatric Association, 2013   2 NHS, 2022   3 Brimo et al. 2021
4 see Melago, 2024 on instrumental teaching

The term 'high functioning autism' (in the past interchangeably used for Asperger syndrome, Level 1) is sometimes utilised for those with average or above average intelligence, but it is not liked by everyone. This is because it was based on intelligence levels (IQ). These are no longer considered a good indicator of functional level. 'Functional level' refers to a person's practical skills for everyday living, for self-care, and their capacity to interact and cope in social situations, etc.[5]

As Sheila Scott observes: 'Some children with ASD function so well that they are difficult to distinguish from their typically developing peers. Other children with ASD are profoundly impacted'.[6] It is important to reiterate that not every case of autism equates to a deficit in intelligence, capacities or human potential, musically or otherwise. People with autism can be of any intelligence,[7] and they may have special interests with high capabilities, including for playing instruments. The latter point is borne out by the autistic savant, Derek Paravicini, who has extraordinary musical talents. (see Ockelford, 2007)

Indicators and the diagnosis of ASD

Issues with *communication* and *social interaction* may include:

- Problems with starting or reacting to conversation, or with understanding cues within it, i.e., when and when not to speak. There may also be difficulties with communicating feelings. Some people with autism may also steer conversations to their particular interest areas when these are not appropriate in the context or at the time. All this assumes the person in question can communicate verbally.[8]
- Inability to comprehend the thoughts and feelings of others (i.e., limited emotional reciprocity and empathy).[9]
- Issues with communicating nonverbally. This may include an inability to maintain eye contact, or trouble using bodily

---

5 see Alvares, 2019
6 Scott, 2017, https://doi.org/10.1093/acprof:oso/9780190606336.001.0001
7 NHS, 2022   8 Scott, 2017   9 NHS, 2022

gestures or facial expressions or with understanding others' use
of them.

- Relationship problems or the inability to maintain relationships.
  Sometimes, there may be difficulties in making friends or
  limited or no interest in having them.
- Taking longer to understand information.[10]

Restricted and repetitive behaviours have been linked to anxiety
levels in individuals with ASD.[11] These may include:

- Demanding consistency in procedures and routines along with
  discomfort when deviating from them. There may be anxieties
  about changing routines and schedules or a very high focus on
  specific activities, thus experiencing problems with switching
  between them.
- Fixation on specific interests or topics, which may be very
  narrow.
- Repetitive, involuntary body movements (e.g., rocking, hand
  flapping, whirling in circles), but in more significant ASD
  conditions.

There may also be *sensitivity to certain sensory circumstances*
including:

- Feeling overwhelmed, stressed, agitated or nervous around
  new people and in new social situations.[12]
- Having trouble adapting, such as e.g., when the music
  classroom is changed, etc.
- Increased or decreased sensitivity to noises, textures, light,
  smells and other sensory input.

Since ASD is a wide, complex spectrum, the above 'indicators' are
neither intended as a comprehensive list nor are they all experienced
by every person. Their emphases will also vary according to the

---

10 NHS, 2022
11 American Psychiatric Association, 2013; Rodgers, Glod, Connolly & McConachie, 2012
12 NHS, 2022

individual. As a case in point, the situation with a particular learner whose ASD is not obvious, Level 1, will be markedly different to someone who has Profound and Multiple Leading Difficulties (PMLDs) *with* ASD. So, '. . . no single educational program[me] meets the needs of all individuals in this diverse population'.[13] In this chapter therefore, the aim is merely to give some general starting points for instrumental teachers to *consider* integrating into their work to innovate germane pedagogies for individual circumstances. Many of the ideas that have been derived from the literature also assume the learner is verbally communicative, and intellectually and physically able to learn a standard instrument.

Another significant point concerns what constitutes an autism diagnosis. There are self-evaluative screening tests employed by healthcare services, such as the Autism Spectrum Quotient (AQ-50).[14] Tests in this vein entail a person ranking statements about his or her experiences and capacities relating to, in the case of the AQ-50, dimensions of 'social skills', 'attention shifting', 'attention to detail' and 'imagination'. Rankings are made on a scale of 'definitely disagree' to 'definitely agree'. A person can score highly for one or more of these aforesaid dimensions whilst not achieving an overall test score large enough for an ASD diagnosis. Accordingly, we might say that some people without ASD regardless have some autism traits.

The benefits of learning an instrument

Music can be helpful for people with ASD in various ways. It is '. . . an emerging practice for targeting [the] language development of young children with ASD'.[15] Playing an instrument can offer opportunities to be engrossed in an activity that plays to strengths. Research has suggested that many people with ASD have acute pitch perception and an affinity with music.[16] Learning a musical instrument is also inherently social, whether on a one-to-one basis or in groups. Group music is '. . . a way to create that base-level

---

13 Scott, 2017, https://doi.org/10.1093/acprof:oso/9780190606336.001.0001
14 Baron-Cohen et al., 2001
15 Vaiouli & Andreou, 2018, p. 324; see the authors' review of evidence
16 Accordino, Comer & Heller, 2007

connectedness between the student, peers, and teacher'.[17] So, providing it is well managed by the teacher, lessons afford a fitting situation for developing skills in appropriate social interactions, including through verbal and non-verbal communication. 'Music . . . offers a safe space for the development of social competencies and, across the spectrum, musical interventions are regarded as an effective way of promoting engagement with others'.[18]

Learning and making music, either in group instrumental lessons or ensembles, can also provide a dependable context for making friends and maintaining those friendships when this is, otherwise, an issue. Indeed, it has been observed that children with ASD enjoy interacting with others through music.[19] Furthermore, regular lessons, home practice and other musical activities can offer a comfortable routine. Derek Polischuk (2016) remarks that, whilst schools are far more challenging for the learner with ASD by requiring socialising in multiple contrasting situations throughout the day, plus by needing to navigate frequent changes e.g., with classes and breaks, etc., the 'private controlled nature of a music lesson can be a comfortable and native environment for a student with High Functioning Autism [sic.]' (p. 16). There may also be advantages for those who participate in group instrumental music:

Because of the nature of music...students find it difficult, if not impossible, to be isolated in a music classroom. ...each student must attend to every other student in the group if the group is to perform successfully. Thus, the music classroom can serve as a nonthreatening environment in which students with autism [along with communication deficits] and their peers can initiate and maintain communication. In fact, the music classroom is probably the only school environment where social and academic integration of these students can occur relatively easily and naturally.[20]

---

17 Wald & Bernstorf, 2024, p. 30   18 Lisboa et al. 2021, p. 1   19 Wan et al., 2010
20 Darrow & Armstrong, 1999, p. 18

The impacts on instrumental learning

Some ASD traits may be advantageous for the instrumental learner. High focus, or even preoccupation on specific tasks that *some* people with ASD have may assist them in building technical competence and making progress. Whilst a non-autistic learner's motivation might wane when encountering repetitious tasks e.g., practising scales or technical exercises for a lengthy time, someone with ASD might well be absorbed in these. Intrinsic motivation, creativity in neurodivergent thinking, hyper-fixation and cognitive immersion are potential assets for musicians with autism.[21] In an online survey of 3,470 people with ASD, their parents and their broader support network,[22] many expressed that descriptions of autism should focus on people's unique qualities. One respondent commented, 'While it is clearly imperative to consider the needs that people with an ASD have, I feel that there also needs to be more of a focus on strengths and differences rather than disabilities'.[23] However, there are also challenges for the teacher, not least:

- The needs of learners who do not immediately appear to have ASD can easily be missed. Teachers can assume they are capable of more than is being produced or fail to identify the requirement of specific teaching strategies.[24]
- The learning aims will go beyond academic or technical growth in music to encompass dealing with '. . . students' abilities to manage their own behaviours to communicate and interact with others, and to gain awareness of themselves . . .' (Scott, 2017).
- Depending on the student, instrumental teachers may need to plan strategies that build in comfortable routines into their lessons as well as managing any necessary change.
- Instrumental teachers must assess how social situations e.g., group instruction, chamber or larger ensembles, might be daunting for participants with ASD. These rest on social interactions but may also present sensory distractions.

---

21 see Tang, 2025   22 Kenny et al., 2016   23 p. 452; cf. Tang, 2025   24 Polischuk, 2016

If instrumental lessons occur within a school, there may be effects from the wider environment, and the student's general organisation and wellbeing needs consideration. Pupils arriving e.g., to the peripatetic music teacher's lessons come primed from their earlier experiences in the school day. As Derek Polischuk (2016) remarks:

> If asked to design an environment specifically geared to stress a person with Asperger's Syndrome [sic.], you would probably come up with something that looked a lot like a school. You would want an overwhelming number of peers; periods of tightly structured time alternating with periods lacking any structure; regular helpings of irritating noise from bells, school mates, band practice, alarms, and crowded, cavernous spaces; countless distractions; a dozen or so daily transitions with a few surprises thrown in now and then; and finally, the piece de resistance: regularly scheduled tours into what can only be described as socialization hell (a.k.a. recess, lunch, gym, and the bus ride to and from school). It's a wonder that so many children with ASD manage to do so well.[25]

Pedagogy

Routines and predictable learning environments

Routines with managed flexibility

Consistency in lesson structure and more widely might be key to catering for music learners with ASD.[26] This has potential for curbing their anxiety, and this must be manageable before they can learn. Essentially, increasing anxiety decreases learning! Minimising change and establishing a more predictable lesson environment may be critical to reducing stress in the learner, resulting in educational advantages.[27] Discussing how the lesson is organised with the learner, where realistic, and with others involved such as paraprofessionals or parents attending lessons (e.g., the overarching lesson structure,

---

25 p. 16; also see Bashe & Kirby, 2001   26 Draper, 2020; cf. Stokes, 2017   27 Williams, 2001

anyone or anything new being introduced, expected behaviour and procedures to manage it, time changes, etc.) are likely to be well worthwhile. It may also be helpful to provide learning materials in advance of lessons. Where the instrumental lesson occurs within schools, consistency in procedures (e.g., behaviour management) might be best made as synchronous as possible with those in other parts of the school day.[28] With some students, this predictability might extend from the overarching structure and sequence of lesson activities to more specific (micro) strategies for embedding kinaesthetic skills even in small parts of pieces.

Teaching case study – Charlotte and Aarav

Charlotte is a piano teacher who delivers online lessons from her home. Her pupil, Aarav is a 17-year-old with ASD. The connotations of Aarav's condition for his communication and learning are consequential. He can communicate verbally and follow instructions but needs substantial support (i.e., Level 2). Aarav has deficits in verbal and nonverbal communication, rarely initiates social interactions and exhibits inflexibility. Accordingly, he attends a mainstream UK secondary school (broadly equivalent to a US high school) where he spends a portion of his time in a Special Educational Needs (SEN) unit. As part of his weekly routine, Aarav has a piano lesson on Thursdays after school with Charlotte. Charlotte has been teaching Aarav using a videoconferencing platform since the Covid-19 pandemic. This is a comfortable routine for him. His mother, Zainab, sits beside Aarav to support Charlotte e.g., with behaviour management.

Aarav is preparing for his Associated Board of the Royal Schools of Music (ABRSM) Grade 6 piano examination. In this lesson, Charlotte and Aarav have completed their usual routine of practising scales first and are now moving onto a piece. The piece is Friderich Kuhlau's 'Allegro', the first movement from Sonatina in C, Op. 20, No. 1. This starts with an Alberti bass in quavers (eighth notes) in its left-hand part.

---

28 Hourigan & Hammel, 2017

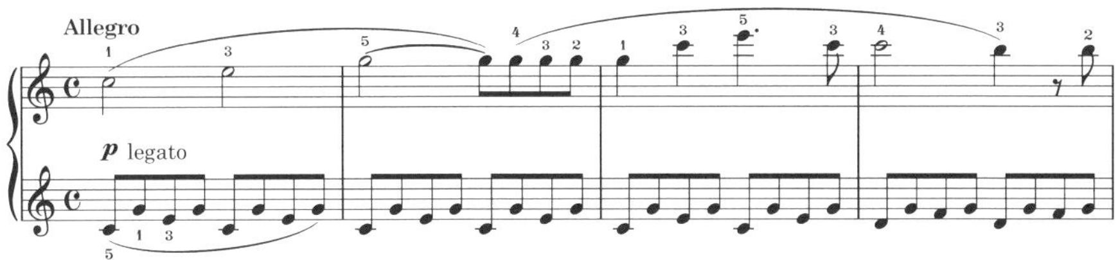

Charlotte (teacher): Aarav, point at the left-hand's stave. What is
    the clef?
Aarav (pupil): Treble.
Charlotte: What is the first note?
Aarav: E.
Charlotte: No. Look again.
Aarav: C.
Charlotte: Put your left hand in its starting position. Finger 5 on
    middle C. Finger 3 on E. Finger 1 on G.

*Aarav moves his fingers into this position correctly. Zainab can be
seen on screen making notes in a notepad.*

Charlotte: Push your fingers down in this order: 5, 1, 3, 1.
Aarav: Now?
Charlotte: Yes.
Zainab: Now, Aarav.

*Aarav plays the figure slowly with the right notes, but with a
hesitation after the E.*

Charlotte: Now, four more times a bit faster like me. All the notes
    the same length.

*Charlotte plays the opening figure whilst simultaneously counting
the beats '1, 2, 3, 4' etc. The piece is in common time. Aarav
repeats playing the figure four times counting '1' for the first,
'2' for the second, etc. By the fourth, his quavers (eighth notes)
have become more even.*

> *Commentary: Charlotte's instructions were favourably direct given Aarav's condition. There was no superfluous language. On a 'macro' level there was also a weekly routine in place, i.e., lessons occurred at a particular time, on a particular weekday and in a particular format (online). On a 'meso' level, the sessions have a consistent outline structure, starting with scales before proceeding to a piece, etc. On a 'micro' level, Aarav has become accustomed to embedding technical skills by repeating figures five times. Charlotte commented that he often pre-empts this practice, i.e., doing it without being asked. Overall, there was consistency here, which is comforting for Aarav. He has been known to show signs of frustration in response to changes. Zainab has been on hand to support Charlotte with behaviour management where needed.*

Educators have also advocated 'picture schedules' or, alternatively, activity plans in text form that can be read through with the student.[29] For instrumental lessons, these plans might be concerned with repertoire and learning activities in the sequence they will be studied. Instrumental teachers might wish to ponder how their lessons can be understood in short, compartmentalised activity periods e.g., a warmup, an examination piece, a technical exercise, scales, aural tests, the student's own choice of piece and a follow-up chat with mum, etc. For younger learners, or those with more severe ASD, 'picture schedules' can be made using Velcro fasteners for fixing picture cards of lesson components to a board in a timeline. This results in a clearly expressed lesson structure, but with notice about what is coming up. That predictability may be reassuring for some children and young people with ASD. Furthermore, this allows for flexibility, and it notifies the student of change, e.g., if a new activity will be introduced or the sequence altered for whatever reason. It may be vital to 'prepare the student for all environmental and/or changes in routine . . .'.[30]

---

29 Hourigan & Hammel, 2017; also see Morena & O'Neil 2000 on 'visual schedules', or Stokes, 2017 on 'clearly written daily schedules'
30 Moreno & O'Neil, 2000

Teaching case study – Leo and Maisie

Maisie has Level 2 ASD. She is 12 years old and learning the clarinet. Maisie has been learning for just over two years with her teacher, Leo. She is doing well. She recently passed her ABRSM Grade 2 examination. The lessons are normally held on Fridays at Maisie's home. Her mother sits in, makes notes, and lends support with motivating and maintaining Maisie's focus.

This week, the lesson is taking place at Leo's home. It is also on a Wednesday in Leo's music room with Maisie's mother waiting in the living room. Leo is going on holiday hence the change in the format and weekday.

Leo (teacher): Let's start with your piece this time.
Maisie (pupil): No.
Leo: It's normally a warmup, but I'd like you to play your piece.
Maisie: No.

As Leo opens Maisie's book, Leo's son enters the music room and wanders around in the background. Maisie's discomfort increases. She turns around to look at him. Leo directs him to leave. He lingers.

Leo: It's a beautifully pensive, melancholic piece, Maisie. Let's see how you play it.

Maisie tentatively starts playing but then stops suddenly shouting "No". She pushes over the music stand, with the music falling on the floor. Maisie's focus shifts to Leo's son again. Leo is shocked.

What went wrong? *There was too much inconsistency and change. The lesson day had changed disrupting Maisie's overall routine. The location and participants were also new. Leo's son wandering around in the room was distracting. Adding to the mix, Leo's emotional language e.g., 'melancholic', was likely confusing to Maisie. The teacher's insistence on starting with the piece might have been less of an issue if signposted ahead of time and the* *only change. However, there was a sea of deviations with which Maisie could not cope. These brought the situation to a head. An early clue of impending disaster occurred when Maisie said "No". Given the lesson day needed to be changed, perhaps careful consideration of what could be controlled might have been prudent.*

Flexibility is paramount. Charlotte (see the case study, 'Charlotte and Aarav' above) also remarked that, sporadically, she needed to be led by Aarav, more so than with other pupils, i.e., when a break was required or where it was best to abandon a particular activity to allay a tantrum. Aarav's mother was helpful in interpreting her son's behaviours in that regard.

Assuming every learner with ASD intuitively knows the next step may be awry. In a competition, he or she, for instance, might not start playing unless told it is part of a required sequence of events.[31] Some may struggle more considerably with their general organisation than others too. Ryan Hourigan and Alice Hammel (2017, p. 24) recommend that a '. . . task analysis is a great way to break down a set of information into small steps for students [with ASD] who struggle with executive functioning and cognitive processing' (p. 24). Table 7 is an adaptation of their ideas.

---

31 Polischuk, 2016

**Table 7. An example task analysis,
adapted from Hourigan and Hammel (2017)**

Preparing to start Richard's trumpet lesson
1   Walk from your school classroom to the instrument cupboard
2   Collect your instrument and music folder
3   Bring the instrument and folder to the instrumental teaching room
4   Wait outside until the teacher's other lesson is finished
5   When the pupil leaves, come into the room
6   Put the folder on the stand
7   Put your trumpet case on the table
8   Open the case
9   Put the mouthpiece into the leadpipe
10   Take your trumpet and stand in front of the stand
11   Do not play
12   Give your teacher a thumbs up

Changing teachers

Changing instrumental teachers is a normal part of the young musician's journey. There are any number of reasons why this might become necessary. For instance, a learner might move home or move to a new school for lessons there. He or she may develop musically beyond the current teacher's skills and abilities. Or a change may come about when the relationship between the various participants is just not working. There can be many reasons. However, this can be more unsettling for students with ASD as opposed to more simply being seen as an entirely positive step. Diane Adreon and Jennifer Stella (2001) have spotlighted the relevance of teacher transition meetings in the US public school system, which allow '. . . the previous instructor to educate the incoming teacher on strategies that have worked for an individual with high functioning autism [sic.]'[32]

Here we should be cognisant of three points. Firstly, ASD does not represent one set of circumstances, so workable strategies will be individualistic and valuable to be shared. Secondly, instrumental teachers may have limited or no training in ASD and thus learn pragmatically through experience within their practices. Brown, Draper and Judith (2022) '. . . found that [music] teachers who were more confident teaching students with ASD were also those who had more undergraduate coursework in special education topics' (p. 54; also see Helps, Newsom-Davis & Callias, 1999 on inadequacies in teacher training). Effective 'handovers' will be very helpful. Thirdly, there may be situations where the learner's condition is so severe that the typical instrumental teacher cannot cope. Nordoff Robbins (2025) is an example organisation in the UK that offers music therapy and associated training programmes for music teachers. It can steer parents towards the right experiences for their child (this charity is also included in the book's directory).

Decluttering and removing sensory distractions

The attention of some instrumental students with more severe ASD conditions may incline towards non-social objects (such as colourful signs, shiny or colourful instruments elsewhere in the room, etc.), that is, rather than towards faces and people's expressions, their body language, etc. For those students, it will be important to remove distractions from sight lines.[33] It may be essential to declutter teaching rooms, therefore, and e.g., avoid any seating changes between lessons if these cause anxiety in the learner.[34] A stable, decluttered environment may help to increase the student's focus on the music activities. Distractions can occur in the peripheral vision e.g., background movement such as people entering and leaving the room, or from other children seen passing by a window. They may well extend beyond the visual, though, to background noise from neighbouring teaching rooms, sounds coming through an open window, or fluorescent lighting humming. Normal auditory and visual input can be perceived both as overwhelming and too little.[35]

---

32 Polischuk, 2016.p. 17   33 Hourigan & Hammel, 2017   34 Moreno & O'Neil, 2000   35 Ibid.

Some considerations for the instrumental teacher
(interim summary):

- *Appreciate* the extensiveness of ASD with its various influences on an individual's cognition, social interaction and communication. There may also be comorbidities.
- *Consider* how instrumental learning can offer some individuals a safe, comfortable routine and environment for social skill development and friendships. Broaden its aims to encompass the learner's wider personal and social development.
- *Plan and express* a consistent, predictable lesson structure.
- *Build* consistency into the instrumental teaching environment (i.e., the physical space), the behaviour management practices and the pedagogy.
- *Declutter* the teaching room and remove sensory distractions.
- *Synchronise* behaviour management strategies with elsewhere in the school, if viable and that is the working context, and seek advice of parents on effective approaches in the home.
- *Reflect* on how change can be carefully managed.
- *Plan* transition meetings when there is a forthcoming change of instrumental teacher so that the incoming teacher understands strategies established as effective.

Language and communication

Concise, literal language

Students with autism may understand language more literally than others, so language needs to be clear, concise and direct. 'Some children [learning music with ASD] who have limited verbal skills can get confused easily with wordy sentences and phrases'.[36] Asking, 'Why did you do that?' might better be reframed as, 'I disliked you banging your fists on the keyboard. Next time, do not bang them. Tell me that you are frustrated'. Ambiguous language such as *'Perhaps you'd like to play those notes smoothly or without gaps'* might also be misunderstood by the learner to be something optional rather than an instruction to be heeded. In this latter example, the 'or' might

---

36 Hourigan & Hourigan, 2009, p. 42.

Table 8. Communication and instrumental learners with autism

Avoid	*Example(s)*
IN LESSONS WITH THE LEARNER	
Long sentences	
Reflective, vague expressions	'What might you do there?' (i.e., when referring to a forte symbol on a score)
Language that might be interpreted to offer options	'Would you like to shut the teaching room door?'
Terms that concern emotion or imagery	'That needs to sound happy', or 'Make that part sad sounding', 'Trudging up the hill'.
Multiple terms for the same concept	'Thirds', 'skips', 'line-to-line', 'space-to-space' (when explaining intervals of a third on stave notation).
Idioms (ibid.)	'You are trying to cut corners with your fingering', 'This part is a piece of cake', 'Let's call it a day', 'Let's throw in the towel with that exercise', 'You need to go the extra mile with your practice', etc.
Sarcasm (ibid.)	'Oh, great' (after hearing the student has forgotten his or her sheet music).
Reliance on non-verbal language	Raising an eyebrow at poor intonation, or a frown at inappropriate behaviour, or smiling at a good performance.
Assuming the student has understood he or she has been successful	

Instead	Example(s)
Concise sentences	
Clear, direct instruction	'Play it louder', or 'That symbol means louder'.
Clear, direct instruction	'Close the teaching room door.'
Clear, direct instruction	'Play it faster and loudly with separated notes', or 'Play it slowly, quietly and smoothly', or 'Play the upward scale and get slower from the lowest to highest note'.
One term per concept	
Avoidance of idioms	
Avoidance of sarcasm	
Verbal language	'Your F was too low', or 'You must not slam the door', or 'You played that well'.
Persistent praise where appropriate, i.e., to alleviate comorbid anxiety disorder	'You played that melody well', 'That was bowed correctly', 'Your posture was good'.

Avoid	*Example(s)*
WITH PARENTS OR IN RELATION TO PARENTS	
Asking the child to relay messages to parents (unless part of the acquisition of a new skill and monitored)	

cause confusion as an additional way of explaining the concept. Similarly, language that links emotion, metaphor or imagery with musical interpretation can be missed by students, for example., 'That needs to sound happy' or 'That melody should soar like a bird'. Moreno and O'Neal (2000) also advise against using multiple terms interchangeably for a single musical concept, to simplify and avoid confusion. Examples might be for a minim (half note) in $\frac{4}{4}$, 'Twice as long as a crotchet (quarter note)' but also 'Half the length of the bar'; or 'This is a viola clef' but also 'an alto clef'; or 'bar' and 'measure'; or 'the harmony' and 'the chords'. These authors (ibid.) also recommend avoiding sarcasm and idioms too. Again, we must recognise that people with ASD will have different capacities and comprehensions as regards language and communication. So, this is general advice to be tailored to the specific student. Table 8 is a starting point for reflection.

Verbalising the non-verbal: Some learners with ASD do not apprehend the gestural aspects of communication well, such as body language, physical gestures and facial expressions. Instrumental teachers use these frequently without much awareness. They smile when something has been played well, raise an eyebrow at poor

Instead	Example(s)
Ask parents/carers about:	their child's cognitive and communicative capabilities, day-to-day strategies used for supporting them, how they are acquiring new skills and learning in other contexts, how to motivate them and manage distraction
Direct communication with parents	

intonation or a frown at inappropriate behaviour, etc. People with ASD can struggle with interpreting body language and reading faces.[37] With some students, the instrumental teacher must not rely on these in place of verbal communication but, instead, be self-aware and give comments that clearly verbalise the non-verbal.

Teaching case study – Freya and Isabella

Isabella has ASD. She attends a mainstream UK primary (elementary) school. Isabella is in Year 6 and is 10 years old. Her class teacher notes that she struggles to follow instructions and loses focus sometimes. Isabella learns the clarinet with Freya during the day at school. This is in the staffroom. She is preoccupied with music, which is 'her thing' and her mother reports that she becomes absorbed in practice. Good progress has been made since she started two years ago. Isabella has quickly developed into an intermediate player.

Isabella is learning a simplified arrangement of Nikolai Rimsky-Korsakov's 'Flight of the Bumblebee', which Freya has engraved

---

[37] Moreno & O'Neal, 2009

for her. Freya is eager to reinforce the work they have been doing recently on chromatic scales and semiquavers (sixteenth notes), so this piece is perfect.

Freya (teacher): The melody flies along, doesn't it, and it's easy to make a mistake. Practise individual bars first, but slowly, before putting them together into longer stretches. Learning it is a journey that you should embrace, really. The melody should sound light and airy, sort of joyful and light-hearted. Start at a snail's pace though.
Isabella (pupil): Do you want me to start?
Freya: Sure, ready when you are.

Isabella doesn't start. She appears distracted by pictures on a noticeboard that is on the wall in front of her stand. Freya prompts her.

Freya: Play it now.

Isabella commences slowly but accelerates rapidly making various pitch errors.

Freya: Okay, that wasn't very good. You'll need to pull your socks up if you want to perform it in assembly. There's more to this piece than meets the eye. Run your eyes over the fingering again and . . .

Isabella starts playing again, which is unexpected as Freya intended to continue with her explanation. Freya appears annoyed by Isabella's inattention.

What went wrong? *Isabella may have struggled with idioms due to her ASD. Apart from being lengthy, Freya's instructions contained many of these. It was her normal spoken style. Thus, Isabella was left in utter puzzlement at how a melody 'flies', how it can be 'light and airy', or how 'eyes can be run over its fingering', or what 'pulling up her socks' has to do with music, etc. Equally, terms that connected music to emotions such as 'joyful' or 'light-*

hearted' were perhaps less meaningful in this instance. Possibly, Isabella would have responded better to more literal instructions, so 'Ready when you are' was confusing to her, although she did start after a clearer prompt. When she did, Isabella seemingly took Freya's instruction to 'Start at a snail's pace' literally too, i.e., to imply that she should subsequently get faster. Very quickly Isabella had potentially found herself in a quagmire of language that she struggled to comprehend. When she started part of the way through her teacher's instruction, this was arguably more about her inability to understand her comments than about poor behaviour.

Clarity on behavioural expectations

Subtle vocal nuances may be missed by some music learners with ASD. These might allude to, for example, irritation when they overstep boundaries or fail to do something they have been told to do. Therefore, explaining one's behavioural expectations to children with ASD and prompt, unswerving implementation of clearly stated consequences, where needed, may make lessons more comprehensible for them. In '. . . inclusive educational settings, it is important to meet their needs in ways that are minimally disruptive to class functioning and that appear normative to their peers' such as with targeted, class-wide management of turn-taking, verbal interactions, etc.[38] All this also adds an additional layer of structure to the teaching sessions, which can be very reassuring for some. However, consistency is key. Children with ASD may respond particularly well to structured discipline because of their need for routine, whereas any drop in consistency may, contrariwise, contribute to unease. Appropriate rewards and consequences (e.g., extra time, or no time on a favourite piece) might, therefore, prove productive. 'Descriptive praise' or 'reprimand' also aids in the child's understanding of one's behavioural expectations, for example, 'Good work *for closing the piano lid gently*', or 'It is bad *that you have forgotten to bring your sheet music* to the lesson'.

---

[38] Weiss & Harris, 2001, p. 794

Praise and reinforcement that encourages risk taking

Owing to comorbid anxiety disorder that occurs in some learners with ASD, they can be risk-averse. This impedes their desire to participate freely and creatively when encountering tasks. Using language that identifies progress such as 'The rhythm was better than your last try' and thus reinforces success at the tasks and challenges may promote positive behaviours. In this regard, '. . . our efforts can create a feeling of safety within the classroom and a positive culture that encourages participation and risk taking'.[39] This means giving students feedback *at the time*, in the context of the lesson, so they can more meaningfully appreciate their progress, rather than relying on follow-up summations (e.g., within end-of-term reports, or in lesson notes shared with parents afterwards).

Don't be put off by music learners with ASD

Initially, the behaviours of some children or adults with more severe cases of ASD can be disconcerting for music educators inexperienced with them. A preoccupation on specific topics can lead them to steer conversations to special interests that seem irrelevant. These digress from the instrumental learning taking place. This can feel disruptive. Similarly, some learners with ASD may fidget or, in more severe cases, engage in stimming. 'Stimming' refers to self-stimulating behaviours such as repetitive body movements. 'Stims' can include hand-flapping, rocking the body back and forth, spinning or head-banging, but they can also include staring at objects or even vocalisations. Tourette's syndrome can also co-occur with autism, which can cause a person to utter involuntary sounds, for example, grunting, whistling, tongue-clicking, repeated phrases or words, or even swearing, etc. There is no evidence to suggest that learners with ASD are not concentrating because of fidgeting or stimming. These behaviours might mean the opposite is true. It may simply be how the person is managing sensory input. Additionally, if the instrumental learner with ASD wants, for example, to bring a comforting fidget toy to his or her lessons, or is reassured

---

39 Hourigan & Hammel, 2017, p. 25

by wearing a hat indoors, or wearing digital earbuds, it is sometimes shrewd to go along with it.

Communication with parents

'Families are essential partners in the education of children with autism'.[40] The parents of children with Special Educational Needs and Disabilities (SEND) can be the instrumental teacher's greatest ally, supporter, resource and guide. Those parents will have knowledge of their child's cognitive and communicative capabilities. They will have extensive 'lived' experience with their child leading to pragmatic day-to-day strategies for supporting them in the household and beyond. Parents will have insights on how their child is acquiring new skills at home, and they may have understandings about how they are learning effectively at school and elsewhere. They can also advise on what motivates their child. They can describe how to manage him or her becoming suddenly distracted. Discussing all this with them can be immensely helpful. Sadly, many parents will have experienced negative incidents too, of their child being excluded, or being pushed from pillar to post, so, when faced with an instrumental specialist who shows a genuine interest, they may be keen to invest personally. That might mean sitting in on lessons or being alongside their child during home practice. Since so much can be gleaned from parents, it is worthwhile having them attend lessons with subsequent discussion a way to learn.

When instrumental lessons occur at school and within the school day, as in the peripatetic work delivered by UK music services, it is unlikely that parents will be able to attend. Moreno and O'Neal (2000) caution it may not be sensible to ask children with ASD to relay messages, either verbally or to carry notes home, unless with a follow up as part of their learning of a new skill. The child may simply forget or lose these. This also applies to any notebooks containing practice details. Perhaps regular telephone calls or emails might be more fruitful, but only if compliant with the school's policy and agreed with parents.

---

40 Azad & Mandell, 2016, p. 435

Some other considerations

Generalisation of concepts

Students with ASD may find generalising skills they learn more troublesome. Accordingly, Brenda Smith Myles and Richard Simpson (2001) recommend a 'scope and sequence' instructional approach. This involves teaching students about 'the specifics', ensuring these are well understood, before addressing the generalised rules. An example would be first learning a scale's fingerings on the piano (the abstract principle) yet understanding that a student might not know instinctively that those same fingerings can be utilised for portions of the same scale in a piece they are learning (the generalised rule).[41] Equally, a violin student with ASD may not intuitively understand that a sequence of up and down bows for a particular rhythmic motif applies to that same motif elsewhere in his or her piece (i.e., where it has different pitches). There is no suggestion here that this does not, to a certain extent, pertain to students without ASD too.

Teaching case study – William and Rhys

Rhys is 16 years old. He has mild ASD (Level 1) with seemingly no impacts on his communication and behaviour. He learns the piano with William who is aware of his SEN.

Following some detailed work, Rhys has mastered a challenging right-hand melodic and rhythmic motif near the start of his piece. It is in the tonic key of D major. William has written the fingering underneath it and demonstrated. The piece has now modulated to the dominant and the motif has appeared again, but at a new transposition.

William (teacher): Okay, start here where the key has changed. This piece is in a major key. How do we work it out?
Rhys (pupil): You look at the sharps at the start [of the staves].
William: Yes, we look at the key signature and, if we have two sharps . . .?

---

41 Polischuk, 2016

Rhys: We go one step above the second one, uh, the one furthest
    to the right.

William: Go on . . .

Rhys: It's in the C space of the treble stave, so D. It's D major.

William: Excellent. Well done. The key has changed here though,
    so what are we looking for to figure it out?

Rhys: Accidentals?

William: What are those?

Rhys: They're sharps or flats next to notes.

William: Where is there one?

Rhys: There is a G-sharp.

William: Great, so we have three sharps: F, C and G-sharp. G is the
    last sharp so what is one above that?

Rhys: A. It's A major.

William: Brilliant. So, start from there right-hand only.

Rhys begins, but his fingering and rhythm goes awry.

William: Music is often made up of things that are repeated, Rhys.
    Can you spot where that happens in this piece?

Rhys: No. Maybe the rhythms?

William: Yes, but also parts of the melody and the fingering. I'll
    show you.

*William draws a box in pencil around the right-hand motif in the
tonic key that Rhys has understood. He also encases the dominant
transposed version in a box.*

William: These are almost the same. The second one is the same
    melody, with the same steps and jumps. It's just the notes are
    shifted higher by the same amount. If that happens, it makes
    sense to use the same fingering, doesn't it?

Rhys: Always?

William: Most of the time. Copying the first box, write the
    fingerings underneath the notes in the second one. I'll get you
    to play it after that.

__Commentary__: William utilised exploratory questions effectively to reinforce his pupil's thought processes in relation to keys and key structures. At least initially, however, Rhys was unable to generalise how his prior knowledge of finger patterns applied elsewhere in the piece. This may have been due to his ASD. Fortunately, William responded quickly by drawing his attention with pencilled boxes and a task i.e., asking Rhys to copy the fingering across from the first to the second box.

Using technology

Digital technologies, for instance the video facility on many smart-phones, can be a good way to give instrumental learners with ASD more time to digest the required executive skills.[42] The authors suggest recording, for example, a video file of a hand playing a scale correctly and sending this to children's parents so that it can be rewound and reviewed as often as required. This strategy was utilised in the lessons delivered by Charlotte, the piano teacher mentioned earlier, but in relation to short passages or melodic lines. A proviso is that educators must be careful that any practices in relation to video or taking photographs for pedagogical reasons are in-keeping *both* with parents' wishes and, if applicable, Child Protection policies in schools.

Set realistic expectations

It is prudent to set realistic expectations for the individual. Some learners and music participants with ASD will be perfectly capable of reading music notation to pursue instrumental grade examinations (as with Aarav above). It is fine, however, that others never achieve perfecting a notated piece of repertoire. Examinations and recitals may be demotivating for some, adding to their stress. Some learners, too, may have extraordinary musical skills and abilities, and others not. Some may best learn aurally i.e., by ear, or through 'participatory styles' of musicking that build social skills (see Chapter 1), while

---

42 Hourigan & Hammel, 2017

those with the most severe conditions and comorbidities, may best be served by specialists and their therapeutic strategies. Sensible expectations are essential, but it is also imperative that the music participation is enriching and meaningful for the learner on some level.

Some considerations for the instrumental teacher
(interim summary):

- *Adjust* your language since students with ASD may be literal, or fail to recognise phrases that link emotion, metaphor and imagery to musical interpretation.
- *Avoid* using multiple terms for the same musical concept.
- *Verbalise* non-verbal communication in music and music-learning (i.e., where the teacher uses body language, physical gestures, or facial expressions).
- *Decide* on behaviour management protocols and be consistent with them with children and young people. Implement appropriate rewards and consequences using 'descriptive praise' and 'descriptive reprimand'.
- *Give* immediate feedback (i.e., as part of the ongoing teacher-pupil lesson interactions). It should explain progress (e.g., against the previous lesson, or in relation to a previous attempt during the lesson, etc.). This may be important for decreasing pupil anxiety and, at the same time, increasing his or her openness to risk taking.
- *Explore* with parents, carers, any paraprofessionals, or SEN specialists and other teachers working with the learner (where possible), effective learning, motivation and management strategies employed in other contexts.
- *Understand* that some learners with ASD may find generalising basic musical concepts and ideas to other situations more difficult. These may need to be clarified.
- *Determine* realistic aims and expectations for the individual. These can vary widely so consult others, where possible, and recognise personal limitations to draw on specialist advisors, or hand over to specialist music educators or therapists if needed.

Reflective questions

- What are the key indicators of ASD?
- What are the benefits of learning an instrument for people with ASD?
- How might consistent and predictable environments, pedagogical strategies and routines be created for instrumental teaching?
- How might communication be different due to ASD?

Suggested further reading

Bakan, M. (2020). *Music and autism: Speaking for ourselves.* Oxford University Press.

Darrow, A.-A., & Armstrong, T. (1999). Research on music and autism: Implications for music educators. *Update: Applications of Research in Music Education 18*(1), 15–20.

Hammel, A. M. & Hourigan, R. M. (2020). *Teaching music to students with autism* (2nd ed.). Oxford University Press.

Honeybourne, V. (2018). *The neurodiverse classroom: A teacher's guide to individual learning needs and how to meet them.* Jessica Kingsley.

Hourigan, R. M., & Hammel, A. M. (2017). Understanding the mind of a student with autism in music class. *Music Educators Journal, 104*(2), 21–26.

Hourigan, R. M., & Hourigan, A. (2009). Teaching music to children with autism: Understandings and perspectives. *Music Educators Journal, 96*(1), 40–45.

Ockelford, A. (2007). *In the key of genius: The extraordinary life of Derek Paravicini.* Hutchinson.

Ockelford, A. (2013). *Music, language and autism: Exceptional strategies for exceptional minds.* Jessica Kingsley.

Polischuk, D. K. (2016). Autism Spectrum Disorder research and its implications for music teachers. *American Music Teacher, 66*(1), 15–18.

Scott, S. (2017). *Music education for children with Autism Spectrum Disorder: A resource for teachers.* Oxford University Press.

4

Visual Disabilities

What is a visual impairment?

'Visually impaired' (as opposed to 'sighted') is used in this book as a blanket term referring to a continuum of conditions from people who are blind (that is, with no light perception) to those who have some functional vision. The person's sight issue cannot be fully rectified, for example, by wearing spectacles or by surgery due to medical, or even economic or geographical reasons. On the latter point, consider the prevalence of cataracts in the developing world.[1] Many are easily resolved with an operation, but sadly medical intervention is inaccessible to a large quantity of people worldwide. Although 'impairment' suggests a deficit, that is, what people *cannot do* (see Chapter 1), it is used here because medical administrations have it as part of their formal registration procedures. 'Visual impairment' is, therefore, a term recognisable by many. Nonetheless, terminology varies across organisations, countries and medical systems, etc. with many different terms employed and sometimes utilised interchangeably: 'blind', 'sightless', 'partially sighted', 'low vision', 'vision loss', etc.

Formal registration as 'visually impaired' normally rests on an assessment of visual acuity and fields. 'Visual acuity' concerns the clarity or sharpness of any vision, so relates to the ability to perceive light, shapes and discern contrast, etc. This is typically assessed with a Snellen test, which is a chart with letter rows descending in size. 'Visual fields' are, by distinction, about the extent or coverage of visual perception when looking straight ahead, including a person's peripheral vision.

At one end of the aforesaid continuum,[2] 'blind' denotes the absence of or negligible light perception that is non-functional. It

---

1 Hashemi et al., 2020   **2** see Baker & Green, 2017

cannot be utilised for daily living. Along this continuum, though, there are people who can use light 'functionally' to navigate, and/or they can perceive shapes, even those of people to hold conversations, etc. At its other end, there are partially sighted people whose vision is functional enough for reading supported by magnification and other assistive technologies. As with other disabilities, there may be comorbidities to consider too. The point at which a person's sight condition occurs is also highly significant (congenitally, in later life, etc.), as are the person's life experiences. Some visually impaired people will be highly confident and adept with assistive technologies, daily life and their independent mobility. Others, however, may be underconfident and highly dependent.

The impacts on instrumental learning

Instrumental learning within classical traditions relies on reading stave notation and, often, sight-reading from it. This is not only encashed in its printed repertoire but also in its associated practices. As a sighted professional trumpet player, for instance, it was normal to arrive for an afternoon orchestral rehearsal where I would be given the sheet music to sight-read before performing in an evening concert. For blind instrumentalists using music braille (see explanation below), their part must be acquired, learned and memorised ahead of time. Learning from it normally means iteratively touching the tactile code then playing small parts until the entire piece is locked into the procedural memory. That takes time. This typically makes sight-reading unfeasible. Alternatively, some blind musicians may opt for musical genres where notation is less dominant (such as some folk or jazz). In that way, they can play by ear and improvise. Those approaches may feel more comfortable and far more inclusive. Others may defer to the 'participatory musicking' described in Chapter 1, perhaps if there are comorbidities preventing access to standard instruments, ensembles and repertoire, or they may be served by music therapy. However, for those with enough vision and cognitive faculty to read a score (and music braille is but one prospect), assistive technologies may be needed. Again, depending on their specific formula, these may take sight-reading out of the equation. For others though, it may be possible to engage in it. Everything depends on the person's eye health and any other conditions, their background and thus experiences with musical media, technologies and approaches, as well as their preferences towards certain music. Aural, tactile and kinaesthetic learning are also brought to the fore. Melcher and Zampini (2011) argue that visually impaired musicians' brains may exhibit consequential differences:

> . . . if one sense is absent [i.e., sight], another sense can take over and involve the neurons in those areas associated with the non-functioning sensory modality. This cortical plasticity may help to explain why blind people have increased auditory (but also tactile) abilities when compared to sighted people (p. 270).

This is not to imply that every visually impaired person will be an innately exceptional musician. Restricted or absent vision can also significantly affect the nature of verbal communication within lessons (as discussed later in this chapter). So, instrumental teachers must be willing to explore and adjust to the raft of possible teaching and learning strategies, materials and technologies.

Benefits of learning an instrument

There is a long history of 'blind musicianship' across Europe, the Middle East, Africa and Asia sometimes connected to heightened spirituality and extraordinary musical capabilities.[3] Straus (2011) remarks that '. . . in popular imagination, blind people are compensated for their disability with preternaturally acute hearing as well as prodigious musical gifts' (p. 170). In ragtime, jazz and soul there have been some superb instrumentalists ranging from the earliest traditions (such as Thomas Bethune a.k.a. 'Blind Tom' Wiggins, 1849–1908, or 'Blind' Lemon Jefferson, 1893–1929)

---

3 see e.g., Baker & Green, 2017; De Ferranti, 2009; Groemer, 2012; Isaki, 1987; Kononenko, 1998; Lubet, 2011; Meeker, 2006; Ottenberg, 1996

to more recent times (Rahsaan Roland Kirk, 1935–77 or, in jazz and gospel, Art Tatum, George Shearing, Ray Charles and Stevie Wonder).[4] In the classical sphere there is the singer Andrea Bocelli and concert pianist Nobuyuki Tsujii.

Instrumental learning offers visually impaired people an opportunity to key into those traditions and their associated lore, with pride in excelling at something that is part of their social history. This often drives non-disabled people's interest in them. The lore and 'othering', contrariwise, have patent disadvantages in terms of identity and inclusion.[5] Music provides an auditory medium too, which can be hugely meaningful. As with non-disabled learners, visually impaired people can benefit from all the creative, cognitive, physical and social benefits of music.[6]

Pedagogy

Understanding assistive technologies, score types and their implications

Braille and its associated technologies

A plethora of 'assistive technologies' are available to visually impaired people. An obvious one is braille. 'Sonographie' or 'night writing' was a tactile system of raised dots on card used for communicating silently on a battlefield at night. It was invented by Nicholas Marie Charles Barbier de la Serre (1767–1841) for the Napoleonic army. However, troops found it challenging to read. Imagine numb fingers feeling card on a cold night. Barbier considered this to have civilian applications too, including addressing illiteracy in the blind. So, in the 19th century, this inspired Louis Braille to develop his version.[7]

Braille consists of cells, each of which can have up to six raised dots (three rows of two). The pattern of the dots indicates a letter. Braille is not a language, but a code used to convey other written languages. Significantly, Louis Braille was an accomplished organist

---

4 see Baker & Green, 2017 for a history
5 see Baker & Green, 2017; Silvers, Wasserman & Mahowald, 1998
6 see Hallam, 2015, and Hallam & Himonides, 2022 for a review of the related research evidence
7 Jiménez, 2009

who held positions at Parisian churches: Église Saint-Nicholas-des-Champs and the Église Saint-Vincent-de-Paul. He created two types of braille code: 'literary braille' (which corresponds to written text) and 'music braille' (corresponding to stave notation). With music braille, the two pairs of dots at the top of the cell indicate the pitch with the bottom row for rhythm (see Figure 3). There are also indications for time and key signatures, the required octave and 'in accord' for polyphony.

Figure 3. Example of music braille code

C major scale in quavers (note the top two rows of each cell)

C	D	E	F	G	A	B
●●	●○	●●	●●	●○	○●	○●
○●	○●	●○	●●	●●	●○	●●
○○	○○	○○	○○	○○	○○	○○

The note C with different rhythmic values (note the lowest row)

C quaver (eighth note)	C crotchet (quarter note)	C minim (half note)	C semibreve or semiquaver depending on context (whole or sixteenth note)
●●	●●	●●	●●
○●	○●	○●	○●
○○	○●	●○	●●

Today, there are also numerous device options that visually impaired people can use with braille (literary and music). There are, for example, braille embossers, which range from small, mechanical typewriter-style hardware devices (e.g., the Perkins Brailler) to modern, digital counterparts. Visually impaired people can also use electronic braille notetakers, which are small, portable devices with tactile keyboards and integral digital memories. Information can be stored on these for reference later or for use with a computer. There are also refreshable braille displays, which plug into the USB ports of personal computers. These interpret the visual elements on computer screens outputting them as tactile braille code on the device. MuseScore music engraving software offers a 'live braille' feature that can be used with one of these. They are often supported by synthetic speech. This synthetic speech (or 'text-to-speech') is generated by software known as a 'screen reader'. Commonplace software programs are JAWS and NVDA.

Teaching case study – Jonathan and Amir

Amir is 17 years old. He has a congenital condition with no functional vision since early childhood. Amir started learning the guitar and piano from age 10 and reads music braille well. His instrumental teacher, Jonathan, does not read it, but has expertise in music technologies. Lessons have included learning and memorising pieces from braille transcriptions and tab, which has been embossed on light card. However, they are also keen to explore Amir's creativity, passion for pop music and his improvisation skills.

Amir has a computer with Digital Audio Workstation (DAW) software installed. This is not specialist software for disabled people. It is mainstream music production software that allows users, for example., to create multi-part MIDI compositions with digital sample libraries. It also enables users to record live performances using a microphone that can be part of their creative productions. Amir accesses his PC with a refreshable braille display, which is a specialist hardware device connected to his computer via USB. He also uses screen reader software. These are specialist pieces of equipment and software designed for visually impaired people. Amir cannot see the visual elements on his computer monitor (e.g., clickable buttons, menus, popup windows, icons, etc.). As he navigates around the DAW software, pins are pushed upwards through holes in the upper surface of his refreshable display rendering braille code that he touches and reads. As this happens, these elements are also read aloud by his screen reader software as synthetic speech. Amir is adept at this and has created a pop track utilising samples for an electric bass, drum kit and piano. Previously, he has recorded a rhythm guitar part too. It is now time to record an improvisation using his MIDI controller keyboard and a synthesiser sound to complete the composition.

Jonathan (teacher): Amir, I'll trigger the recording. You'll hear four clicks before you start playing.

Amir makes his first attempt but gets lost with the chord structure of the piece. He plays several wrong notes. Amir grimaces and Jonathan stops the recording.

Amir (pupil): I'm getting lost.
Jonathan: No problem. Let's do some work without the backing first.
Amir: Okay.
Jonathan: It's the same as a turnaround cycle in a 12-bar blues progression in G major. So, where you're getting stuck is where there are half bars of B minor, E major, A minor, D major.
Amir: I remember learning that before.
Jonathan: Good, so play me those chords with your right hand in that order. Don't worry about the rhythm. We can add that in later and talk about the other notes needed to make an improvised melody.

Amir finds the B minor chord, then E major, but hesitates with A minor.

Amir: Oops.
Jonathan: I'm going to guide your fingers, Amir. Is that okay?
Amir: Fine.
Jonathan: Play that again.

Amir begins again but, at the A minor chord, plays (bottom to top) B (thumb, right hand), E and A.

Jonathan: Freeze!

*Jonathan gently lifts Amir's thumb onto the C. Amir confirms
he has understood and tries again, this time getting the sequence
right.*

Jonathan: I'll start your composition for you to play against. Just
improvise using those notes and hand positions. You can decide
on the rhythm. It won't sound great, but it'll be good practice so
that, when we add to it, you don't get lost.

*They record and listen back to Amir's attempts, discussing any
errors. At times, Jonathan guides Amir's fingers to the right place,
and he demonstrates on the MIDI keyboard too. Over time, Amir
navigates the harmony more competently and they begin to
discuss and test additional notes that could be included, such
as sevenths, blues notes, etc.*

*Commentary: Assistive technologies were allowing Amir to
explore his musical interests, which was motivational. This was
also creative. Additionally, Jonathan and Amir had found a way
in which the technologies could be utilised to support Amir's
instrumental learning through recording himself, listening, self-
appraisal, and dialogue. However, employing technologies in
this way relied on Amir having experience in them for general
computing. Not all visually impaired children would have that. This
was a supplementary approach for Amir, as he also learned pieces
from embossed music braille.*

People with visual impairments use braille and its associated devices
in many fascinating ways to communicate, read and write about
music, learn about it and make it. Since braille is such a distinctive
system, it often springs into many people's minds in relation to blind
musicians. Non-disabled people are, understandably, fascinated
by it and how those musicians learn or compose music. However,
there are some key points for instrumental teachers to bear in mind:

Music braille use will be low per capita amongst visually impaired instrumental learners.

Published research even shows that the numbers of literary braille readers are small.[8] As visual impairment represents a vast range of sensory conditions, a misconception is that visually impaired people are always without functional vision and, therefore, braille is the only suitable reading medium (for text and music). Some can access stave notation (for example, using magnification on a computer or tablet).

Music braille is neither quick nor straightforward to learn.

Learning music braille takes time and considerable effort. It is an entirely different experience for someone who learned it from a specialist teacher beginning as a young child compared to another who, after losing his or her sight, attempts it in adulthood. Even for the aforesaid young child, it may be difficult to find a suitable music braille instructor in his or her geographical area (if there is one).

Braille scores may not exist presently or take time to acquire. Stave notation can be transcribed into the code. However, obtaining pieces will hinge on, for example, the music braille libraries of charities like the Royal National Institute of Blind People, or on commercial transcription services. There are also some automated software transcription services such as GOODFEEL from Dancing Dots (a US business that sells assistive technologies). These can generate music braille from MIDI files or MusicXML, saving them as digital braille (.brf). Access is set to improve through the efforts of organisations like The DAISY Consortium.[9]

Learning from music braille is dissimilar to using standard stave notation.

As mentioned earlier, the iterative (touch then play), tactile process of memorising pieces from braille (perhaps cross-referencing

---

8 see e.g., on the UK and US: Keil & Clunies-Ross, 2002; Morris & Smith, 2008; Park & Kim, 2014
9 DAISY Consortium, 2025

with audio) is labour intensive, slower and typically makes sight-reading impossible. A few exceptions to this exist. In the Arts and Humanities Research Council (AHRC) 'Visually impaired musicians' lives' project,[10] there was a research interviewee who performed in a choir. She described sight-reading from braille as she performed.

Using music braille challenges participation in some musical genres and performing contexts.

It is imaginable that an instrumentalist using music braille might rehearse and perform in an ensemble alongside sighted peers who read stave notation parts. We may consider this ethical too, so that e.g., a child or young person can enjoy a school orchestra or band. There would be inclusiveness, and social and educational benefits. However, our European traditions of music often rely on sight-reading, which, as explained above, may prove impractical. So, this means ordering a transcribed music braille part (which takes extra time) with that student subsequently memorising it ahead of his or her rehearsal (the same). This requires careful planning as well as the cooperation of ensemble directors who understand the situation.

Decisions need to be made if music braille is the instrumental learner's current medium, or if they feel strongly that it is important.

Instrumental teachers without the facility to read it may need to decide either to learn it, which is challenging,[11] or to defer to a specialist teacher. There are specialists in dedicated music schools. Examples include the Academy of Music for the Blind (AMB, 2025) and the Filomen D'Agostino Greenberg Music School (FMDG, 2025) in the US, or the Toronto Institute of Music for the Blind, Canada (TIMB, 2023). National charities may also be able to point to suitably skilled teachers (see the *Directory* at the end of this book). Examples include RNIB's music team (RNIB, 2025a, b) and the Amber Trust (2025) in the UK, the American Foundation for the Blind (AFB, 2025), the Canadian National Institute for the Blind (CNIB, 2025),

---

10 Baker & Green, 2017
11 for introductory and other books, see e.g., Krolick, 1998, Spanner, 2023, Wesseling, 2004

Blind Citizens Australia (2025) and Blind Low Vision New Zealand (Blind Low Vision NZ, 2025). Then there are special schools and colleges too (as examples, in the UK, Linden Lodge School, London, and the Royal National College for the Blind, Hereford, or, in the US, Perkins School for the Blind, Watertown, Massachusetts) who might be networked with music braille teachers. Qualified Teachers of the Visually Impaired (QVTIs) in UK schools may also be able aware of music braille teachers. Defaulting to an expert is, arguably, a sensible step if approached by an intermediate and advanced instrumental learner already competent in reading music braille. In any case, the instrumental teacher should clarify what he or she can contribute, perhaps by supplementing music lessons taken with a braille specialist.

Teaching case study – Danielle and Camila

Camila is 17 years old. She is an accomplished soprano and aspires to audition for a music conservatoire. Camila reads music braille and acquires this from transcription services. The text and music are represented on two parallel lines of embossed code, the upper one for the words and the lower one for the music. Her singing teacher, Danielle has developed a basic understanding of how music braille works but is far from fluent. Her understanding is visual, so she can identify note names and rhythms by sight only.

Camila has recently received her transcription for 'Caro nome' from Giuseppi Verdi's Rigoletto. *She has wanted to learn this aria and has a CD recording.*

Danielle (teacher): It's taken a while to get this [braille transcription], hasn't it?

Camila (pupil): I haven't had much time with it yet.

Danielle: Let's give the recitativo a go. It's marked 'Allegro assia moderato'. What does that mean?

Camila: Fast but very moderate.

Danielle: Yes, so not too fast and there's a *morendo* at the end, so, as Gilda sings 'core innamorato' you slow down and let it die away. There's lots of pulling and pushing with the tempo in this part.

Camila feels her score. The lyrics are translated into English.

Camila: I've got English words.
Danielle: Let's do this in Italian. I've got it here on my score and
    you've also got the CD. Find the first notes.
Camila: Es? After that C sharps.
Danielle: Yes, I'll sing it first and you copy me. Gilda's singing
    'Gualtier Maldè, his name is so beloved. You carve yourself into
    my heart of love'.

*Accompanying herself on the piano, Danielle sings 'Gualtier Maldè,
nome di lui sì amato. Ti scolpisci nel core innamorato'. Camila
repeats this.*

Danielle: When you get home, I'd practise this by listening to the
    CD first. You can check the notes against your braille. I'd work
    through it bit by bit. I'd sing it in the original Italian. It's a shame
    about the English, but you'll know what the song is about.
Camila: What's going on in this part of the opera?
Danielle: Why don't you find a libretto online and find out? Gualtier
    Maldè is not who he seems.

*Commentary: Danielle was not a fluent music braille reader,
and that did not matter, at least not in this instance. Camila had
been supported in braille reading by a supplementary teacher
with whom she was also studying. She clearly had a level of
competence with the medium to engage with the learning
materials. One point to note however, is that there is perhaps a
balance to be struck between reading music and learning by ear.
Danielle's approach was to engage Camila in listening to a CD or
in performing by copying her modelling, with the braille score very
much in the background. Camila was learning the piece effectively
in this way, but it likely would not have a significant part to play
in improving her music reading and theoretical understanding.
This was a constraint in terms of what Danielle could offer as the
teacher. However, Danielle was able to contribute meaningfully
even so. Her invitation for Camila to discover the context of*

the song online, using her screen reader software, afforded this student with interest in the opera and ownership of the knowledge she would acquire.

Visual scores and their assistive technologies

Aside from music braille, visually impaired musicians learn from various other score formats. Examples include:

- Enlarged stave notation (either printed or displayed onscreen digitally, including photo-enlargements)
- Modified stave notation[12] where elements are adjusted (such as the background colour, thickness of stave lines, note-head size, the vertical and horizontal spacing of elements, etc.) and software such as Dorico, MuseScore or Sibelius, facilitating this

Enlarged or 'large print' notation is used by some. However, there are limits to how large a score can become before the scale of paper sheets or light card, perhaps flopping on a music stand, make it too unwieldy. Additionally, photocopying older, plate-engraved stave notation parts can result in low-quality enlargements with poor, black-to-white contrast. There are digital technologies that display magnified stave notation scores on e.g., tablets. However, displaying just a few bars onscreen, before prompting the next ones with a foot pedal, renders anticipation and normal visual tracking across the score demanding if not impossible.

Talking scores

Talking scores are another option. They are audio descriptions of stave notation, hence extremely laborious for the instrumental learner to digest: for example, 'A5, quaver (eighth note), C, crotchet (quarter note)' sometimes uttered alongside excerpts of the music being played. The Talking Scores[13] website also converts a score in .xml format (MusicXML) into a text file that can be read aloud by a screen reader. It is also possible to access a spoken account of

---

12 see e.g., Zimmermann, 2005   **13** Talking Scores, 2025

stave notation in music engraving software using a screen reader (see above).

Accessing scores

Accessing scores visually can be achieved with a range of available assistive technologies, including:

- Zooming, colour and high contrast options built into Windows or Mac computer operating systems and web browsers
- Specialist magnification software for computing, or hand-held optical or digital magnification devices
- 'CCTVs', which are large table-top machines with a tray where a score can be placed to magnify it (these are not portable)

Indeed, there are many assistive technologies, scores (and score adaptations) and potential learning procedures for the visually impaired instrumentalist. When approached by a new instrumental learner who is already underway with a particular strategy, teachers will need to investigate to understand it and its implications. If starting off a beginner with no prior approach, the support and guidance of music specialists within key organisations, or conversations with specialist technology retailers (such as Dancing Dots in the US), may be particularly enlightening (also see the *Directory*).

Teaching case study – Alexander and Sorcha

Sorcha is an adult learner. She has recently retired. Sorcha learned the bassoon as a child and, after many years, is starting to play it again. Sorcha's visual acuity is deteriorating, but she remembers how to read stave notation. She can access this on a screen with substantial magnification. Sorcha and her teacher Alexander are accessing pieces with music engraving software, a specialist magnification program, and a large (36-inch) computer monitor. However, the necessary magnification means that only a few bars can be shown on the screen at a time. Thus, Sorcha reads, plays and memorises a few notes before moving onto the next set. After memorising a number of these, she puts longer stretches of the music together playing from memory. It is laborious.

Sorcha is preparing for her first performance at church. She is understandably nervous about memorising an entire piece and potentially forgetting part of it.

Alex (teacher): I think memorising the whole piece is a great idea. It's what classical soloists often do anyway. We'll need to think of a way that you can get a prompt if you get lost.

Sorcha (pupil): Yes, and I can't take the computer to the church. (laughs)

Alexander: Perhaps we can print this out [the sheet music], but large. We could glue it onto some backing card so that it doesn't flop and put it across two music stands.

Sorcha: Might work. I'd need to see how readable it is.

Alexander: It might just give you a safety net if absolutely needed. That could make you more comfortable. You'd still need to memorise the piece.

Sorcha: Let's give it a go. My sight's getting worse, so we'll have to revisit the idea of tablet technologies, or I'll need to consider doing everything by ear.

Commentary: The solution that was proposed might be sensible for a while. However, Sorcha's sight is getting worse, causing issues with the accessibility of stave notation. She is at a crossroads. Sorcha has not always been visually impaired. Understandably then, she preferred reading stave notation. Technologies were assisting her in continuing with it for now. However, Sorcha's approach already rests heavily on memorisation. This throws up barriers to ensemble participation where that entails stave notation, i.e., she would need to memorise her parts ahead of rehearsals. Any future step away from notation towards abandoning scores and thus purely learning by ear will have profound implications for the genres, styles and traditions of music in which she engages.

Notation or no notation? Musical pathways

Blind musicians' historical backcloth of assumed 'special dispensations' and 'innate abilities', plus notation being of less importance or not used at all in some of the traditions, can lead people into certain beliefs. It might too easily be supposed that learning and playing by ear is the only, or most appropriate way forward. Partly, this is getting on the bandwagon with the surrounding lore (as we all can do); and part of it is due to insufficient knowledge of the available ways of accessing scores. There is an important question for the instrumental teacher about the long-term connotations of deciding not to support visually impaired students with some form of notation reading (such as braille, talking scores, stave notation, etc.). This may affect their learner's capacity to participate in certain genres, ensembles and contexts in the future. After all, the instrumentalist who has only ever learned by ear sits more comfortably within a jazz or folk group than a symphony orchestra. As Crichton (1992) observes '. . . too often, disabled people have had their experiences decided for them, sometimes by other people's limiting and negative assumptions of what is possible'.[14]

A quandary here is that busy, pressured instrumental teachers barely have time for short-term planning and thinking beyond the next instrumental grade examination, so perhaps they seldom ponder the implications for their students into the long term. Yet, with learners with Special Educational Needs and Disabilities (SEND), those decisions anchor into matters of social integration and inclusion.

Some considerations for the instrumental teacher
(interim summary):

- *Converse* with learners about their sensory perception, *where possible*, and their caregivers, and its connotations for learning music. Some comorbidities may prevent engagement with standard instruments (see Chapter 6) and notation-based

---

14 pp. 213–14

learning. Teaching and learning strategies should be *suitable for the individual*. This discussion might also include wider matters, for example, of dependent and independent mobility and getting to lessons.

- *Avoid* the assumption that music braille is the only solution to musical literacy. It is one possibility, but other score types, technologies and solutions exist. Music braille is also challenging to learn. Transcriptions of music parts take time to acquire and may incur a cost.
- *Explore* the various score options, music-making and assistive technologies that can be deployed (see this chapter).
- *Develop* strategies for aural, tactile and kinaesthetic learning.
- *Contemplate* the implications of not teaching music-reading for the learner's lifelong music engagement. Assess how the selected approach fits with the learner's aims, desires and capacities.
- *Appreciate* that sight-reading might be challenged, or made impossible, by the person's specific condition(s) and resultant music-learning formula (including assistive technologies and/ or adapted score materials). Provide learning materials in good time ahead of lessons and other music-making experiences.
- *Liaise* with specialists in charities and national organisations for visual impairment for advice and support.

Themes in effective teaching and learning

As part of the 2013–15 'Visually impaired musicians' lives' research project,[15] instrumental and class music teachers were interviewed and observed working with their visually impaired students. Some of these were visually impaired themselves. They were asked what they thought were fundamental considerations in music teaching. They included teachers at 'blind schools' and specialist colleges (such as the Royal National College for the Blind, Hereford, the Royal Blind School, Edinburgh, etc.), and instrumental teachers working in private practice. Five themes were identified:

---

15 Baker & Green, 2017

- Differentiation
- Light, position, orientation
- Verbalising gesture, non-verbal communication and events
- Metaphorical language
- Tactile and kinaesthetic learning

These are guiding themes only. It seems apt to revisit a point from the opening chapter that, due to the immense diversity in SEND circumstances, we should be wary of packages of supposedly 'correct' pedagogies applicable to all. These are preliminary ideas to spur consideration only.

Differentiation

There is a distinction between *educational equality* and *educational equity*. Educational equality means giving all learners, with SEND or non-disabled, and regardless of their capacities and backgrounds, the same pedagogies, lessons, materials, resources and assessments. The thinking is that, since everyone is provided with the same, this is fair. Accordingly, no guilt is required of the educational system if a learner fails a test or gets left behind. After all, they have been given the same as everyone else. This perspective overlooks that all humans are inherently unique and, therefore, have different support needs to facilitate fair chances to achieve in line with the relevant yardsticks or tests society puts in place. The perspective also neglects that tests and examinations can only be structured to appraise certain things in certain ways, whilst, at the same time, leaving out other things. So, a particular test may not fit well with a particular student's sensory circumstances, background or how he or she best learns. Thoughtful instrumental educators are aware that, for some children, the differences for engendering a level playing field are small whereas, for others, there are larger distinctions in how they need to be supported and scaffolded.

Educational equity, by contrast, is appreciating that, to give everyone a fair chance of attaining, approaches must be modified and resources channelled to cater for different learner groups or even individuals. This is fairer but, undeniably, tremendously challenging. For governments and educational policymakers it means, for example, distributing funding, resources and even training experiences variously. For music examination boards it means altering assessments or putting in place reasonable adjustments and mitigations for those with SEND. Sometimes music boards give more time and rest periods in examinations, provide more accessible testing materials, have step-free access to examination rooms, or allow a reader or scribe, etc. For teachers, equity means, for example, tailoring instructional practices, adjusting learning tasks and materials, altering how they assess students and attuning learning aims to the individual, etc. Differentiated teaching, learning and assessment are integral to a more equitable educational worldview. In developed countries today, most adept instrumental teachers, class music teachers, ensemble directors, community music leaders and many others, will consider it imperative regardless of whether they are accommodating musicians with SEND or not.

Teaching case study – Ewan

Ewan is a blind adult. As a child, he had a brain tumour that affected his optic nerves. He has no light perception. Ewan took private instrumental lessons in guitar and piano starting at the age of 8. Music quickly became a lifelong passion. He attended a US high school where he learned alongside sighted pupils. Fortunately, Ewan has a gregarious, confident personality so was constantly able to articulate his needs. He is now a successful rock musician and recording engineer. He runs a recording studio and has collaborated with some well-known US rock and pop artists.

Interviewer: There are some massive, massive decisions to be made when you encounter a child [as an instrumental teacher] for the first time, you know, right at the start of their journey. These are around whether you teach them to read [music notation], or you say, 'It's all by ear'. It's about whether you try to engage them in braille or not. These sorts of things, twenty years on, have connotations for the type of music they can engage with. I'm just trying to understand what the teacher does.

Ewan: Well, there's only a finite amount of time. As you know, the teacher doesn't have the ability to spend as much time as might be needed for each student, and each student is going to have a different requirement. So, I don't think it's any different from the basic challenges if you've got 20 kids and you're trying to teach them all the same music. I think the challenge is just magnified when it's a disabled student because the basic communication tools are different . . . It is a complicated question. I think the real question, at the end of the day, is, you know, 'How personalised of a music programme can you have for each student?' The question there is time.

Interviewer: What if it's a one-to-one lesson?

Ewan: I think there's a huge difference because . . . That's why I did supplement my official school [music] classwork with private instrumental lessons to help work on the classwork. . . . I did supplement things I was having difficulty with by having private lessons. . . . The point is that, when you have that private, one-to-one lesson, you can meet those individual goals much more easily because you can tailor goals and how they are met.

Commentary: *Ewan rightly acknowledged the challenges for music teachers differentiating for learners in groups and considered additional complexity when this includes disabled children. He argued that the central question was about the time that teachers had to create tailored approaches. Ewan also noted the importance of one-to-one private instrumental instruction in his story, which afforded individualised approaches and goals.*

A conceivable barrier to differentiating effectively comes from our own musician biographies. We have deeply engrained, personal values surrounding music and how it is to be learned. Simply put, inexperienced instrumental teachers are, understandably, inclined to teach how they were taught (effective or not).[16] This may be particularly so for newcomers straight from undergraduate music

---

16 e.g., Button, 2010; Holdhus, Murphy & Espeland, 2021; Oleson & Hora, 2014

degrees (those with limited pedagogical or SEND training) or those teachers working in isolation. It is inevitable, however, that initial encounters with our pupils' diverse needs is surprising to us. It leads us up a pathway to realising that what worked for us as children does not apply to everyone. Table 9 offers some prompts for the instrumental teacher's contemplation of equality versus equity.

Table 9. Equality versus equity in instrumental teaching

Educational equality *(non-differentiated)*	*Equity* *(differentiated)*
AIMS	
The same aims for the learning apply to every student	Aims are negotiated with each student
PEDAGOGY AND LESSON CONTENT	
The same pedagogy is used for every student 'Presentational' music is the focus, which is deemed suitable for all (see Chapter 1)	Pedagogies are designed for individuals 'Presentational' or 'participatory' music may be studied depending on the learner's capacities and aims
Every student is expected to read stave notation similarly (and to sight-read it)	Different score types may be used and ways of processing them (or no score used)
Students all learn with the same physical materials in the same way (all the teacher's one-to-one students, or all those comprising a group)	There are differences in e.g., score types, associated devices and technologies being used, etc.
The expectations for technique (including posture, instrument holding) are always the same	There are sometimes health-related circumstances where adaptations or adjustments are acceptable (e.g., to posture, instrument holding, or the use of adapted instruments)

COMMUNICATION	
The teacher communicates with every student and his or her parents or guardians in much the same way (verbally, in writing, etc.)	Adjustments are made to how the teacher communicates with individual students (e.g., where a child with attention deficit needs extra reminders, or where aspects of lessons 'seen' by others need to be verbalised for a blind child in a group, etc.)
PLANNING, PROGRESS AND ASSESSMENT	
Lesson planning is the same regardless of the student being taught, or the composition of the group	Lesson planning is shaped by individual students' needs and their distinct approaches
Lesson planning is more straightforward	Lesson planning is more complicated
Learners are expected to accomplish learning repertoire, or parts thereof, or other tasks, for a timescale thought the norm	It is accepted the SEN and its differentiated approaches (i.e., the extra time it takes to absorb and learn) will lead to different expected timescales for progress for individuals
The same examination or test is given to every student	Reasonable adjustments are made to tests and examinations (e.g., extra time, rest periods, accessible test designs and materials, accessible examination rooms, a reader, scribe, chaperone, etc.)
Progress is best measured by external assessment (a curriculum, syllabus, formal examination), which is considered suitable for every learner	Formal examinations or tests may not be appropriate for some students (e.g., depending on aims and their health circumstances)

Differentiating for instrumentalists with visual impairments is complex and requires understanding of:

- learners' capacities, skills and potential in relation to their sensory perception and any health comorbidities (thus setting reasonable aims)
- their backgrounds and wider lives, and how these affect music learning (e.g., resultant confidence levels, mobility [dependent, independent], financial pressures, or the strain of extra time needed to learn other school subjects, etc.)
- prior learning methods that have been used effectively and others open to them
- the most appropriate strategy given their health condition(s) and expressed desires, if they can express them (e.g., notation-based, aural learning, a mixture of both and the required balance, presentational or participatory music, etc.)
- suitable adapted materials that might come into play (e.g., adapted scores, large print, music braille transcriptions, etc.) and how these can be created or sourced
- both assistive and general music technologies that might be utilised (e.g., Digital Audio Workstations, braille displays, embossers, magnification, etc.)
- how best to communicate (see later in this chapter)
- assessment adaptations and mitigations
- and even the physical environment (e.g., the teaching space, trip hazards and obstructions, or how the learner gets to the lesson)

Louisa Maddison was Head of Music at the Royal Blind School in Edinburgh (a UK special school) during the 'Visually impaired musicians' lives' project. She led groups of children with a range of visual impairments along with comorbid autism and physical disabilities. One pupil was a wheelchair user, for instance. Louisa remarked:

I think knowing about the different visual impairments straightaway [when I was a new teacher] would have been very useful. There are so many different types and, with some pupils, if you present an instrument below their chin, they can't see it. If you hold it to the side, they can. If you have five partially sighted people in the class, if you treat them all similarly, you could be doing a big disservice... Every pupil is different, and they are accessing things differently, or working in different ways. You might have two pupils using braille, one using large print, one using audio . . .

Discussions are worthwhile at the first lesson on how teaching and learning have been conducted previously. Some learners can articulate their needs with parents and other caregivers, who are also helpful if learners are uncommunicative or largely non-verbal, for example, where they have comorbid learning disabilities. This brings the instrumental teacher up to speed with the general strategies and materials that have been effective, as well as identifying alternatives. As the lessons proceed, it seems sensible to revisit the discussions from time to time.

Where the instrumental learning occurs in a group context amongst sighted peers, there can be benefits on both sides. If the apt modus operandi is weighted towards playing and learning by ear (alongside notation in some form), then sighted pupils may also benefit. They may profit from the memorisation and internalisation of the musical material. At the same time, the visually impaired participant feels included. Similarly, if the direction is, instead, towards participatory modes of musicking (without notation) (see Chapter 1), these are designed to be more inclusive thus having the same effect.

Instrumental teachers might also show consideration by using the same repertoire with visually impaired learners as with others in a group situation but in alternative formats. Thus, they are not made to feel non-conforming, a problem, or embarrassed. However, this may require careful thought on how scores can be delivered in those alternative formats. For instance, getting a braille part from a transcription service can take time and, likely, there will be a cost involved. Equally, producing a large print or modified stave notation version using engraving software is additional work. In both cases, the student will need extra time to absorb the material, so delivering it to him or her ahead of lessons is wise.

Light, position, orientation

Seemingly paradoxically, light, that is, its direction and intensity, can easily assist or generate problems for some visually impaired instrumental learners. Notably, many *do* have some vision, whether functional or non-functional light perception. We would all agree how problematic it is to place an instrumental student without a visual impairment in a position where strong sunlight is shining into his or her eyes. Orientation in the music teaching space can be equally pressing for visually impaired people. Then, there is the matter of the learner's visual fields, that is, if they are using sight, with, for example, some having reduced fields, or viewing their music and teacher better from one side, etc. At the Royal Blind School in Edinburgh, Scotland, a young instrumentalist was observed sitting diagonally sideways on her chair in an ensemble for this reason. Her teacher was standing in front of the group. Furthermore, some eye health conditions come with photophobia and, therefore, discomfort with strong light, such as uveitis or ocular albinism. For some too, reflections on glossy paper (including scores), or on any whiteboards being used, may be obstructive. When visual acuity means that good contrast is essential, strong sunlight suddenly shining through the back of a paper score, particularly with poor quality engravings, can confound. This can be easily forgotten about by a teacher with good sight who can cope with these. The Royal National Institute of Blind People (RNIB) write:

> Seeing the teacher, who maybe anywhere in the room, seeing other children in your performing group, seeing the instrument you are playing and being aware of the reactions of those just listening are all part of music-making in school. That is all before the winter sun streams in through half of the room... For those with some useful vision, finding the best position for the most important of these is essential. Look out for odd body posture and tension that might be avoided by, say, sitting in the best lit part of the room or close

to the teacher's workstation. Have a music stand with a hard back . . . (RNIB, 2013, p. 6).

Ultimately, detailed comprehension of the visually impaired learner's condition and onward monitoring may guarantee he or she is best positioned within rooms, orientated correctly and the lighting is suitable. Table 10 summarises the discussion:

Table 10. Considering light in the teaching space

	Consideration	*Decisions*
THE STUDENT	No light perception (blind) or some (non-functional or functional vision)	Ascertain
	Vision that is used for navigating and/or music-making	Identify if and how light can potentially cause issues
ENVIRONMENT (i.e., the teaching room)	General light levels	Add or remove artificial lighting, turn up or down dimmer switches, use window blinds, change to a more suitable room, etc.
	Student position and orientation in relation to light sources	Reposition the student
	Student position and orientation in relation to the teacher	Change position, minimise teacher movement around the room
	Light entering from windows	Use blinds or curtains, reposition the student

MATERIALS (e.g., scores, whiteboards, notes in text form, etc.)	Translucence, contrast	Reposition the music stand, use thicker paper or paper with backing card, consider scores with higher contrast printing or digital scores
	Reflections	Employ alternative or matt resources

Verbalising gesture, non-verbal communication and events

Instrumental teachers, instrumentalists, conductors and others involved in music constantly gesture. Sometimes this is a sub-conscious musical practice that has been embedded in us through our experience as musicians over many years; but, at other times, it is more deliberate. Physical gesture is characteristically part of learning and making music. Conductors gesture with their arms, hands, torsos and faces, not merely to convey tempo, pulse and metre but to indicate performance style and dynamics, etc. Ensemble performers use bodily movements, for example, to start phrases together, or to synchronise rhythm, tempo and tempo changes, to be coherent in interpretation and to end chords together in their ensemble sections.

Occasionally, instrumental teachers conduct to guide their students in their performances, or use bodily gesture as they perform alongside them, but they might also, for example, point at notation, nod or smile in approval of their student's attempt, or wince at poor intonation or a split note, etc. However, gesture in instrumental music teaching extends beyond accuracy with notation, and its style and interpretation. Gesture is an equal part of typical human social interaction (beyond music) so that someone can communicate how a behaviour has been received. Equally, gesture conveys how a person's actions fit within norms. Much of this is instinctive, even down to subtle body language signalling when to speak in a conversation. Music educators do this too, to encourage good behaviour, such as frowning when an instrumental student forgets his or her notebook, or a raised eyebrow at a 'tall tale' concerning home practice that has not happened, etc.

Now, imagine for a moment that you are a blind or partially sighted instrumental student and either cannot see these aforesaid gestures or, alternatively, wrestle with seeing them. Perhaps you have some vision, but your visual fields are limited, your acuity is low and sightlines mean your teacher and music group peers are not so easily seen. A substantial amount of vital information can be missed creating a great deal of uncertainty. It might also be that there have been longer term consequences for your personal development due to your interactions with others over time beyond the lesson context affecting your awareness of behavioural norms and social skills. This is rather unsettling for everyone involved. When performing in public too, you might reasonably have anxieties about stage craft such as worrying about whether you are appropriately dressed, or whether your performance gestures appear in line with those typically expected. It is reasonable to expect that your self-confidence may be low.

This seemingly sets up a very demanding situation. However, in one sense, the solution is very simple: verbalise the non-verbal. Verbalisation fills gaps in the visually impaired learners' understanding, and it clarifies otherwise missed occurrences during lessons, thus it reduces uncertainty. It makes lessons clearer and more engaging possibly leading to greater confidence. It is, nonetheless, hard for instrumental teachers to be self-aware enough about those non-verbal aspects of their work, and their life more generally, that are deeply rooted. This is something that may develop with time and experience. One idea might be to engage in co-teaching, peer observations, or mentorship, so that a colleague can feed back on one's communication. Table 11 provides some features of instrumental lessons that might be verbalised with examples.

Teaching case study – Rebecca and Adam

Adam is a 12-year-old who learns the violin in a group of four at his UK mainstream secondary school (broadly equivalent to a US public high school). He is the only one who has a visual impairment. Adam has retinopathy of prematurity with light perception that helps him to navigate with a white cane. Adam has no apparent comorbidities. He is a bright child who is eager to participate and learn. His visual acuity means that, with some difficulty, he can read stave notation with digital magnification, but this takes time to digest, and he mainly relies on music braille. Adam learns from this before lessons to memorise his music. His teacher, Rebecca, has been supportive by getting braille transcriptions in good time. She is understanding about his situation. Rebecca is relatively new to teaching instrumental students with visual impairments.

Rebecca points at the score, remarking 'Go from here'. She utters '. . . and 1' as she begins to conduct an anticipatory $\frac{4}{4}$ bar to lead in the children. The children start playing but Adam starts slightly later than the other children, seemingly catching up and guessing some of the notes before his performance finally becomes more stable. As the children play, Rebecca comments 'Shape the dynamics in the phrase like this' as she moves her arm and hand in the air vertically to indicate changes in dynamic. Adam does not seem to respond to this when they play, at least initially.

What went wrong? Rebecca relied too much on gesture alone, for example, pointing, to locate the point on the stave notation at which she wanted the group to start. This meant that Adam did not know where they were starting and, since he felt embarrassed amongst peers to question the teacher's approach, kept silent. This was compounded when Rebecca conducted a pre-emptive bar to coordinate the children in commencing their performance. Adam was left to guess, so started late, and, initially, he relied on his ears alone to attempt to match with the other children. Eventually, Adam realised which part of the piece they were doing, as he had memorised this from braille previously, and his pitching

Table 11. Some aspects of instrumental lessons to verbalise

Aspect	*Avoid*	***Verbalise*** *(to remove uncertainties for the visually impaired learner)*
Style and interpretation	Relying on gesturing (e.g., with one's hand in the air, or with bodily gestures whilst modelling a performance)	'Join together those *legato* notes so that there are no gaps between them', or 'Increase the volume as you ascend to the highest note of the phrase then let it decrease again' (but, in both cases, model by performing)
Correctness and incorrectness of rhythm, pitch, tempo, dynamics, etc.	Relying on e.g., smiling, nodding, frowning, wincing, other physical gestures, etc.	'The second note is a D, but you played a C', or 'Your Ds are flat so tighten your embouchure and give good breath support like we discussed' (but do model)
Desirable and undesirable behaviour	As above	'Well done, you performed that phrase very accurately in rhythm and pitch this time' (be explicit and descriptive about the behaviour), or 'You must not get up from the piano stool without asking first'

The behaviour of others in a group	As above	'Adam, I am telling Martin off because he threw his sheet music on the floor'
Where to start on a score	Pointing (e.g., 'Start here' whilst pointing)	'Now start again at the third bar of your piece'
When to start playing, and stop	Conducting an upbeat and downbeat with one's hand, or gesturing the same with one's head, etc.	'I'll count you in, so 1, 2, 3, 4 . . .', or '. . . 2, 3, 4, stop'
What others are doing, e.g., within the lesson, or who is entering or leaving the room (reducing uncertainty)	Disregarding this cannot be seen, or might not be seen easily	'The person who opened the practice room door was the school secretary delivering a message. She has now left'
Stage craft	Assuming the learner will know about its norms and, if he or she does, will not need confirmation they are approaching stage craft correctly	'You walked to the right part of the stage, looked great, and how you moved as you performed communicated well with the audience'

*and rhythm, therefore, became more stable. Adam had not got as
far as the dynamic changes at home so, when Rebecca gestured
this with her arm and hand, he could not see what she meant and
again was playing a 'game of catchup' by listening to what the
other instrumentalists were doing.*

Metaphorical language

Humans habitually express their experiences by connecting their
senses. Synaesthesia, for example, is a phenomenon where one
sense triggers another, for example, with the key of a piece of music
inducing sensations of a colour. However, we also use metaphorical
devices in language to link things to our other senses rather than
merely utilising the primary sense through which they are *directly*
perceived. Sound can be described as 'bright', 'warm' or 'dark', or
we might hear a 'sharp crack', or express a colour as 'heavy', or,
indeed, we might feel pleasured by a 'sweet smell', etc. Musicians
employ language in this way (see Table 12 for examples). Again,
this is entrenched in us through experiences and social interactions
over time and it is often unconsciously reproduced. We might
even find ourselves using the metaphorical language of our own
instrumental teachers.

We should recognise the potential effects of this linguistic
phenomenon for a person if one of his or her senses (in this case,
vision) is absent or relatively absent. This is particularly so for those
with severe congenital visual impairments who, conceivably, can
have limited or no experience of apprehending life through sight.
The point here is not that every visually impaired person will have
significant deficits in understanding metaphors, as some will have
experience through sight, or, where not, have picked up meaning
over time. Rather, this is an area to be considered judiciously,
particularly with some children in some cases. It is best discussed
with those children, with their understanding confirmed rather than
assumed.

Table 12. Example musical metaphors

Example	Non-primary sense
'Melody that moves up or down'	Spatial (vertical plane)
'Going up stepwise'	Spatial (motion, vertical plane)
'Angular melody'	Visual, tactile (shape)
'Dark timbre'	Visual (light intensity)
'Deep texture'	Spatial (vertical plane)
'Bright tone', 'Dark tone'	Visual (light intensity)
'Warm sound'	Thermo-reception (temperature)
'More force' (i.e., meaning louder)	Tactile (kinaesthetic)
'Flowing'	Visual (motion)
'Sharply pointed notes' (staccato accented)	Visual, tactile (shape)
'Hopping from one note to the next like a kangaroo' (staccato), 'Like a bird soaring' (melodic character)	Visual (knowledge of the motion of those animals)

Some repertoire also rests on grand metaphors. Programmatic repertoire intends to evoke, for example, a scene, a character or characters, or a narrative. There are some instances of this from the Baroque era such as Vivaldi's *The Four Seasons* (1725), but this came to the fore in the 19th century with, for example, Beethoven's Symphony No. 6 ('Pastoral') (1808), and then in what became known as the 'symphonic poem' with examples being Berlioz's *Symphonie Fantastique* (1830), Mussorgsky's *Pictures at an Exhibition* (1874) or Rimsky-Korsakov's *Scheherazade* (1888), which was based on the Arabian Nights. This tradition also continued into the 20th century with, for example, Vaughan Williams' *The Lark Ascending* (1920) or motion picture soundtracks, for instance, by John Williams (including *Jaws* [1975] and *Star Wars* [1977]). These have leitmotifs representing and announcing the impending arrival of key characters in their story (respectively the great white shark or Darth Vader, etc.). Large-scale works with strongly characteristic melodic, textural and harmonic journeys give powerful impressions of places, situations, people and stories that both performers and audiences are expected to discern. However, the imaginative 'hook' for the creation of repertoire is also present in solo and chamber repertoire, and even in pieces for novice instrumental students. As a few examples, The Associated Board of the Royal Schools of Music's (ABRSM) examination syllabus for 2025 and 2026 includes Dmitry Kabalevsky's 'Gallop/hopping', No. 18 from *24 Little Pieces*, Op. 39 (Grade 2), Florence Price's 'The Goblin and the Mosquito' (Grade 4), and William Alwyn's 'The Sea is Angry' (Grade 5). These expect that children can exploit their imaginative resources by drawing on things they have witnessed – galloping horses, the seemingly erratic, rapid direction changes of mosquitos, or the sea in a storm. However, some visually impaired learners will not have seen such things, so there may be gaps in understanding to be bridged through discussion and creativity.

Teaching case study – Antoine and Amy

Amy is a beginner pianist. She is 9 years old and blind (no light perception). Amy has been learning a piece called 'The galloping horse' that her teacher, Antoine has composed for her. Although he has produced a stave notation score, which has been placed on the music stand, Amy has been gradually absorbing the material by ear. This has been a process of Antoine playing small parts of the music at first (component lines or small figures) with Amy repeating them, receiving instructions, and finally putting together the memorised ingredients into a performance. Her performance is now coherent, so Antoine now wants her to concentrate on style. Amy has never seen a horse but has heard about them from friends.

Antoine (teacher): Galloping is when a horse moves quickly with a particular gait.
Amy (pupil): What is a gait?
Antoine: A gait is how it moves its legs. Amy, turn towards me. Can I hold your wrists?

Antoine gently takes Amy's hands by the wrists. He has previously sought permission from Amy's parents to touch and manipulate her hands fingers and arms, for example, to illustrate fingering, technique or to adjust her posture.

Antoine: Now, relax your elbows, make fists, and make your arms floppy. I'm going to move them for you. I'll show you how the legs of a galloping horse move. Many of your repeated rhythms are a crotchet (quarter note) followed by two quavers (eighth notes).

Antoine sings this repeated rhythm, stressing the first note in each figure, as he bounces Amy's hands in time: left, left, right, left, left, right, left, left, right, left, etc.

Amy: Oh, I get it.
Antoine: This is a large, powerful animal. It's got strong muscles. Your arms were relaxed so I could move them. Let's make the piece sound more like the horse.

Commentary: Antoine attempted to close the conceptual gap here with a simple use of Amy's kinaesthetic sense. In doing so, Amy may have a better understanding of the evocative nature of the piece, which represented an animal she had never seen.

Tactile and kinaesthetic learning

Tactile and kinaesthetic learning have been central to numerous music pedagogies, notably the eurythmics of Émile Jaques-Dalcroze (1865–1950). All music learning can benefit from being multisensory. However, multisensory learning is crucial in the absence (or relative absence) of sight. 'Tactile' refers to our sense of touch. Consider a visually impaired instrumental learner feeling an object, its shape or texture, subsequently relating this to musical material (to appreciate, for example, what 'angular' means in relation to a melody). Alternatively, consider a brass teacher gently tapping that same student's palm to explicate how the tongue moves to articulate certain notes. 'Kinaesthetic', by distinction, refers to a person's awareness of the motion (direction, speed), position, balance and spatial positioning in relation to parts of their body. This comes from proprioceptors, sensory receptors in our muscles, joints and tendons working in tandem with the vestibular system of our inner ear.

Drawing on these aforesaid aspects of learners' sensory perception can aid with embedding the abstracts in music. This can be creatively adopted for musical style (e.g., *staccato*, *legato*, accented, etc.), structural elements in music (such as rhythms, melodic material) or technical practices (posture, etc.). Antoine used this mode of instruction with Amy (see above), with kinaesthesia as a hook for discourse about performance style and the horse.

The Academy of Music for the Blind, California (AMB, 2025) was formed with the support of Ray Charles. Its Founder, David Pinto (2014), has remarked that since visually impaired learners:

> ... can't see others playing their instruments, they can't 'model' their technique on any visual example. Therefore, a teacher must often physically show the musician correct finger, hand, arm and torso positions and use of the corresponding muscles. Although some blind individuals may develop a good technique instinctively, a good, sighted teacher can always help them . . .[17]

Teaching case study – Ewan

Ewan's profile was described earlier in this chapter. In this instance, he discusses his childhood guitar lessons with a treasured teacher.

Interviewer: I'm just thinking about, you know, putting your
    fingers in the right place on the fretboard for an E7 chord.
    To what extent does that need to be much more of a tactile
    experience . . .

---

17 Pinto, D. (2014, January 20). Devoted to teaching music to the blind: Interview with David Pinto, Executive Director of Academy of Music for the Blind. The Epoch Times. http://www.theepochtimes.com/n2/arts-entertainment/blind-music-instruction-academy-david-pinto-26744.html

Ewan: Yeah, it had to be very tactile 'cause fingering is everything. If you finger things incorrectly, you're going to make your transitions sloppy. He was real big on making sure my fingers were curved, not flat, so there was a lot of tactile work. . . . He would say to me 'In root position, you're going to put your third finger on the third fret, fifth string. You're going to put your second finger on the second fret, fourth string. The third string is open, then you're going to put your first finger on the first fret, second string. The first string is open. And you're going to play that from bottom to top as if you're strumming.' So, he would tell me and then he would also have me feel his hands, so we would sit across from each other. He would show me 'This is how I want you to arch your hands. This is where I want you to put your thumb.' So, it was very tactile.

Interviewer: I guess that issue of being tactile is about the fingers on the fretboard but it's also about what you are doing with your right hand.

Ewan: Absolutely! So, we would focus on the left hand, then we'd focus on the right hand. So, we would focus on the different . . . Again, this is why the classical pieces were so important. He'd say 'This is an arpeggio. You're going to play these fingers and these strings one after another' and then 'This is a chord so you're going to play these.' . . . Maybe you'd be asked to pluck them or maybe you'd strum them. So, yes, we would work on both. The first thing I would learn is the shape of the chord or the shape of the melody. We'd get the left hand right and then we'd work on the right hand . . .

Commentary: Several pedagogical elements were present in Ewan's account. He underscored the importance of clear technical descriptions both in relation to navigating the guitar fretboard and technical aspects such as having curved fingers. These were intentionally paired with tactile experiences, including touching his teacher's hands. Furthermore, the learning was compartmentalised into manageable areas of attention: addressing the left and, subsequently, the right hand.

Some considerations for the instrumental teacher
(interim summary):

- *Understand* your role in supporting an educationally equitable
  approach (i.e., through personal adaptation to new aims,
  pedagogies, materials and any technologies required, etc.).
  Differentiate starting with students as individuals.
- *Learn* about prior teaching and learning strategies that have
  been effective and ineffective.
- *Position and orientate* oneself and the learner (considering
  their sensory condition) so that light, its direction and intensity,
  do not disrupt. Ensure light levels are suitable. Remember that
  light can affect the learning materials too (e.g., reflections,
  translucence, glare).
- *Consider* how the metaphorical language used when discussing
  music may have connotations for the instrumental learner's
  understanding (this assumes the learner in question does not
  have a severe comorbid learning disability).
- *Verbalise* the non-verbal aspects of communication (e.g.,
  physical gestures, facial expressions) and other events to
  reduce learner uncertainty.
- *Seek* ways to build tactile and kinaesthetic learning into lessons.

Reflective questions

- How might the aims and strategies of instrumental learning vary
  according to the visually impaired person's sensory perception,
  any co-occurring conditions and their experiences?
- What is the distinction between educational equality and
  equity? How might differentiation feature in teaching?
- What score types and technologies are available?
- How is communication within lessons different?
- What advantageous tactile and kinaesthetic strategies can you
  devise?

Suggested further reading

Baker, D. (2021). Additional needs and disability in musical learning: Issues and pedagogical considerations. In D. Hodges, & A. Creech (Eds.), *Routledge international handbook of music psychology in education and the community* (pp. 351–366). Routledge.

Baker, D., & Green, L. (2016). Perceptions of schooling, pedagogy and notation in the lives of visually impaired musicians. *Research Studies in Music Education, 38*(2), 193–219.

Baker, D., & Green, L. (2017). *Insights in sound: Visually impaired musicians' lives and learning.* Routledge.

Baker, D., & Green, L. (2018). Disability arts and visually impaired musicians in the community. In L. Higgins, & B.-L. Bartleet (Eds.), *Oxford handbook of community music*. Oxford and New York: Oxford University Press.

Castle, C. L., Greasley, A. E., & Burland, K. (2022). The musical experiences of adults with Severe Sight Impairment: An interpretative phenomenological analysis. *Music & Science, 5*, 1–19.

Ockelford, A., Pring, L., Welch, G., & Treffert, D. (2006). *Focus on music: Exploring the musical interests and abilities of blind and partially sighted children and young people with septo-optic dysplasia*. Institute of Education, University of London.

Rowden, T. (2009). *The songs of blind folk: African American musicians and the cultures of blindness*. Liverpool University Press.

5

Auditory Disabilities

d/Deaf people, both children and adults, can benefit greatly from musical participation and learning an instrument (see Chapter 1 for an explanation of 'd/Deaf'). This chapter offers considerations and pedagogical ideas for them. However, this assumes no significant comorbidities or serious intellectual impairments (as in, for example, those with Profound and Multiple Learning Difficulties [PMLDs]). We might imagine that music is not a meaningful activity for people with this sensory impairment, but that is incorrect. Research has shown that many d/Deaf people consider music an important part of their lives.[1] There are also examples of historically significant composers with adventitious hearing loss such as Beethoven and Smetana. Additionally, various pop and rock musicians experienced hearing loss due to noise exposure such as Ozzy Osborne or Pete Townshend of The Who. Although these composers and pop musicians had memory of music ahead of the decline in their auditory capacities, there are also accomplished performers today whose sensory impairment was either present at birth or occurred in childhood, for example, pianist and composer, Danny Lane, or the percussionist and composer Evelyn Glennie. People across a broad range of sensory circumstances can listen to music, appreciate it, compose and perform it.

There are two main types of deafness: *conductive deafness*, or an issue with the outer or middle ear, both of which conduct sound to the eardrum, and *perceptive (or sensori-neural) deafness*, or damage to the inner ear and/or cochlea. As Helen Williams (1989) writes:

Hearing-impaired people will not always hear every subtle modulation and permutation of scoring, but this need not

---

1 Darrow, 1993

remove their 'personal interest' from the music. Many normally hearing but musically untrained people gain enormous pleasure from listening to music without . . . hearing or understanding all that it contains (p. 96).

d/Deaf learners' experiences of playing instruments will be appreciably different to others', however. This includes:

- their way of accessing sound, including through any assistive devices used (e.g., hearing aids or cochlear implants)
- how they perceive sound
- how their sensory circumstances shape music as intersensory experience (perhaps by feeling the vibrations of the instrument they are playing)
- suitable pedagogies for them

The benefits of learning an instrument

Research points to many advantages of instrumental learning for those with auditory disabilities. These encompass social skill gains in children, but also language development, better speech and improved enunciation due to the critical listening involved in playing an instrument.[2] It is also possible that age-related auditory decline is mitigated by musical training.[3] So, this plainly endorses older people's participation with musical instruments. For children and adults alike, there are obvious lifelong connotations for inclusion and enjoyment across a range of music contexts, both within and outside formal education.[4] As with other Special Educational Needs and Disabilities (SEND), those with auditory disabilities can benefit from many of the health and wellbeing profits music offers.[5] 'Although [it]...may seem incongruous, many deaf children and adults do enjoy music'.[6] Paul Gouge (1990) writes:

---

2 e.g., Cheng et al., 2018; Robbins & Robbins, 1980; Schraer-Joiner, 2014; Silvestre & Valero, 2005; Wisbey, 1980
3 e.g., Parbery-Clark, Strait, Anderson, Hittner & Kraus, 2011   **4** see e.g., de Berruecos, 1967
5 see Chapter 7   **6** Fahey & Berkenshaw, 1972, p. 44

. . . if there is any 'handicap' [sic.] to music for young deaf people it is not one imposed by a hearing loss. It is, rather, those wasted years without access to musical experience of whatever sort and the consequent lack of opportunity to build up all the meanings and associations we have towards music (p. 280).

Sound, assistive technologies and music

Many d/Deaf people do have sensation of sound through their auditory system.[7] Many people also communicate through spoken language, but with differing consequences for conversational speech, communication and music. Furthermore, some benefit from assistive devices such as hearing aids or cochlear implants. Some use these for music listening[8] or in their roles as musicians.[9]

Hearing aids and cochlear implants

Hearing aids amplify quieter sounds so that the signal is kept within a comfortable dynamic range. Learners with a more severe hearing disability may have cochlear implants instead. These are an external processor device worn behind the ear coupled with a receiver and electrode package surgically implanted into the inner ear. The external device converts sounds to an electrical signal, which is subsequently sent to the internal receiver to stimulate the wearer's nerves.

Sonic complications

A central point is that these assistive devices are primarily designed for speech. Speech and music are markedly different in their volume, dynamic range (the range from the quietest to loudest sounds), pitch range and their frequency spectra. There is a distinction made here between the term 'pitch range', which refers to the lowest

---

7 see e.g., Akeroyd & Munro, 2024 on the UK   **8** Greasley, Crook & Fulford, 2020
9 Swan et al., 2023

to highest note on an instrument, and 'frequency spectrum', whereby any given note is a complex wave containing more than one frequency (with the combined frequencies dictating timbre). Owing to the limitations of hearing aids designed for speech, the received frequency, timbral and dynamic range information may be limited.[10] Hearing aids may also have an automatic volume control too, which is designed as a protection against sudden loud noises. This can distort music. Clearly, the assistive device wearer will not experience music in the same way. However, some hearing aids have multiple programs; it may be possible to select one that is better for music. An audiologist might be able to help with this. In the UK, Hearing Aids for Music (University of Leeds) can also advise (see the Directory at the end of this book).

Fact-finding and advice

Lyn Schraer-Joiner (2014) recommends starting d/Deaf children's music lessons with a fact-finding mission:

> . . . the music teacher should first embark on a fact-finding mission. This should entail communicating with the appropriate school faculty [where that is the teaching context], staff [the same], and parents. . . . Parents know their child better than anyone and will therefore be able to provide a well-rounded picture of the child's academic and social strengths and weaknesses, as well as his or her musical interests. Music teachers may find that parents are enthusiastic about their inquiries and therefore very willing to describe the musical behaviours that their child has exhibited at home.[11]

Instrument selection

Not all d/Deaf people will use an assistive device like the ones described above. They too will perceive sounds differently. For those who do use an assistive technology though, there is a

---

10 on cochlear implants and music, see Hsiao & Gfeller, 2012   11 Schraer-Joiner, 2014, p. 84

complex interplay of: the specific device's capacity to capture and relay particular sounds, how that relates to the characteristics of the musical instrument being learned (with the trumpet's frequency spectra, range and volume significantly different to that of a double bass, as one example), and how the specific instrument fits within a music ensemble or group learning context acoustically. Learners with hearing disabilities, depending on their specific circumstances, will hear the nuances of certain instruments more easily, and that applies even to those with the most cutting-edge hearing aid technology. Some research also suggests that sustaining instruments offer better aural feedback to learners than percussive ones.[12] The notable percussionist Evelyn Glennie perhaps serves as a counterexample.

When selecting an instrument for the first time, it may be helpful for learners to explore a wide variety of instruments (amongst different instrumental ranges and groups) to discover what works best. Some learners may have strong preferences for an instrument ahead of trying them, which should be taken on board, but through exploration they may become more convinced of a suitable option.

The teaching space, and the teacher and learners within it

Instrumental teachers experience constraints regarding where they can teach. For example, a peripatetic (travelling) instrumental teacher visiting schools will likely be offered a particular room, or the rooms available will inevitably be limited. However, when teaching children with auditory disabilities, it is wise to avoid reverberative rooms, or those with an echo or background noise. Sometimes, high ceilings and hard surfaces can be mitigated by dampening with curtains. In some schools, it may be possible to select a room that is further from a noisy classroom, or from a neighbouring room with a thin partition wall where another loud instrument is being practised. For instrumental teachers working in their own homes, moving instrumental lessons from, for example, a kitchen with its

---

12 see e.g., Darrow, 1989

tiling and hard surfaces to a living room with its soft furnishings may help. Trial and error and discussion with learners may pay dividends.

Learners engaged in large-group or whole-class instrumental lessons are sometimes split into subgroups to practise together or for creative enterprises such as generating compositions together or improvising. However, if this is done in a shared space (such as a school hall) this may be disconcerting for a d/Deaf child who is included. That learner may struggle to isolate the sounds of their group from those of others. Sending groups into separate break-out rooms might be more effective.

When working with inclusive instrumental groups in larger spaces, the teacher should find a position where he or she is close enough and clearly visible to any d/Deaf learner. However, this should be done tactfully and without singling out, for example, by placing him or her in front of a class or in an odd ensemble arrangement compared to non-disabled peers. Medium-sized instrumental groups might also stand or sit in semi-circles to ensure that everyone, the d/Deaf learner included, can see everyone else i.e., so that musical and verbal communication is enhanced. In larger spaces, the teacher might move closer to the learner without moving him or her to a strange ensemble position that causes embarrassment.

Teaching case study – Noah, Bethany, Andrew and Amelia

Bethany is in UK Year 6 and is 10 years old. After her visiting instrumental teacher, Noah, performed in an assembly at her primary (elementary) school, she became eager to start cornet lessons. Bethany's 20-minute weekly lessons take place in a group of four children. Since lesson costs are subsidised by the school's budget, the headteacher insists they are organised in groups for cost effectiveness. This is a small, village school and the hall is the only available teaching space today. Aside from its other hard surfaces, it has wooden flooring; the acoustic is very reverberative. Bethany wears hearing aids.

Only one child, Andrew, has remembered to leave class, collect his instrument and sheet music, and arrive on time for the lesson in the school hall. Noah is feeling pressured and has sent Andrew

*back to collect the other three children, two from another class,
including Bethany who has forgotten. The four children arrive
5 minutes later than scheduled, which is quite a feat even so, and
he is now keen to get them organised quickly as he needs to drive
to his next school in a timely manner.*

Noah (teacher): Quick. Get your instruments out of your cases and
    stand in a row in front of the music stand.
Amelia (pupil): I've left my music in class.
Noah: You can use Bethany's.
Amelia: Do I need to go back to class to get it?
Noah: Not if you're using Bethany's.

*As this exchange between Amelia and Noah happens, Andrew
starts playing a warm-up from the previous week. It is a lip slur
exercise alternating between Cs and Gs. Another child, Edward,
has taken his mouthpiece out of his case, but not his instrument,
and is slapping with his palm to make popping noises.*

Noah: Stop that, Edward. Pick up your instrument and do what
    I said. Everyone, join in with Andrew's warm-up.
Bethany: Can I go to class with Amelia to get her music?

*Partway through Bethany's question, the other children have
joined in with the warm-up. She then joins them just before Noah
indicates for them to stop.*

What went wrong? *The problems with this lesson vignette related
to its circumstances and context. The children arriving late along
with the time pressures that a busy peripatetic instrumental
teacher often experiences led Noah to become flustered. As a
result, he did not manage the behaviour of the group particularly
well. A reverberative environment within a school and disparate,
overlapping sound sources, made it difficult for Bethany to follow
what is going on. Noah seemed unaware of the implications of
this. If persistent, it may hinder Bethany's progress but also affect
her motivation over time.*

Some considerations for the instrumental teacher
(interim summary):

- *Explore* a variety of instruments (with different pitch ranges and timbral qualities) if possible when assisting the learner to select one.
- *Avoid* reverberative rooms – those with an echo or background noise. Consider dampening or teaching in rooms with soft furnishings.
- *Use* breakout rooms when splitting large groups of instrumentalists into subgroups for any creative tasks.
- *Avoid* moving learners with SEND to unorthodox ensemble positions, or into atypical positions in group music lessons.
- *Arrange* medium-sized instrumental groups in a semi-circle to facilitate musical and verbal communication without singling out the individual.

Pedagogy

Sound separation

d/Deaf learners may encounter additional challenges in separating sounds. Instrumental teachers may need to avoid giving verbal directions and feedback whilst the learner is playing or when other music is heard, either performed by others in a group setting or whilst listening to a CD of a backing track or recorded music example. Listening to music is vital in any instrumental lesson but listen first and *subsequently* explain. In group teaching too, where a d/Deaf learner is included, this will necessitate skilled behaviour management to ensure young instrumentalists understand the need and do not talk or play at inappropriate times. Moreover, if the teacher is leading an ensemble that includes a d/Deaf participant, a protocol for tuning his or her instrument may need to be agreed.

Using audio devices

Setting audio device levels carefully may be crucial. If using a digital device to play an audio track, for example, to listen to the piece being studied, or for a backing track, it is sensible to check the volume is comfortable for the d/Deaf instrumental learner.

A multisensory curriculum that begins with simple melodies

Owing to challenges the d/Deaf learner may have in separating out one sound from another, it is also advisable to start beginners with simple melodies. A curriculum of repertoire can then add musical complexity, but in a steady progression. This may seem obvious for all instrumental learners such as those with auditory disabilities or non-disabled, but it is easier for hearing aid wearers or those with cochlear implants to listen to single instruments or melody lines. Musical complexity, in terms of melodies with accompaniments, multiple lines or counterpoints, backing audio, or more complex textures, can be added over time. Some evidence[13] also suggests d/Deaf learners may be more responsive to rhythmic dimensions of music than tonal ones. Accordingly, melodies for beginners might need to be carefully selected without complicated melodic contours.

Hearing impaired learners may also perform more accurately from notation than by ear (see Darrow, 1989). This is because music notation includes supplementary visual information relating to pitch and note duration utilised as part of a multisensory experience. So, whilst momentarily abandoning stave notation undoubtedly has aural learning benefits for non-disabled beginner instrumentalists, it may, contrariwise, have some drawbacks for d/Deaf people. Teachers might wish to experiment with other graphic representations of pitch and duration too. We should be mindful that if a well-meaning teacher remarks, for example, "I'll play a melody that is not on your score. Repeat it", this may hold more significant challenges for the hearing disabled beginner than expected. d/Deaf

---

13 see Darrow, 1989

learners bring into play multisensory or 'multimodal' strategies[14] whereby learners experience music through their other sensory modalities. These call into question the primacy of hearing[15] in our musical encounters. Sutela and Ahonen (2024) explain:

> Sound – and, thus, music – can be experienced in multiple ways . . . without valuing one sense over another. . . . Not using this powerful ready-made tool in music learning and teaching is not just exclusionary but is unsustainable for music education...we suggest that music educators pay attention to tactile, visual, and kinaesthetic ways of teaching music.[16]

Multisensory approaches are established by research.[17] As learning progresses, the teacher should constantly monitor the learner's sensory experience.

Teaching case study – Arlo and Liam

Liam is 11 years old. He has his trumpet lessons in the village hall opposite his UK primary school. His teacher, Arlo, collects him from class and takes him there for a 30-minute lesson each week. Liam relies on hearing aids as he cannot discern some sounds and lip reads for conversation. An interpreter does not accompany him to lessons. He took to the trumpet as, out of the brass instruments on offer, it seemed to have the frequency range and volume he could hear best.

Arlo has used a low tack tape to mark white lines across the floor of the room. These represent a melody in C major in a graphic score, with the length of each line (left to right) for the note durations and the distance away from Liam's feet their pitches (lower to higher). Just above Liam's toes is the starting note, which is a C. He was intrigued when Arlo got a roll of tape from his instrument case and started marking the floor.

---

14 Schraer-Joiner, 2014, p. 89   15 Palmer et al., 2017; Palmer & Ojala, 2022
16 Sutela and Ahonen, 2024, https://doi.org/10.1177/1321103X231223864
17 e.g., Bang, 2009; Darrow, 1993, 2003; McCord & Fitzgerald, 2006; Silvestri & Hartman, 2022

Liam: What are you doing?

Arlo: Step onto the line above your feet. It's the first note you are
    going to play.

Liam: What now?

Arlo: Step sideways twice. It's a minim [half note] so two beats.
    Now step up onto the next note. Do the same. That's also
    two beats.

Liam: It's one step, one note higher, right?

Arlo: Yes.

Liam does this correctly.

Arlo: Yes. This time do both notes and I'll clap. You'll need to step
    sideways each time twice in time with me.

Liam: That's hard.

*Liam keeps his movements approximately in time with Arlo's
clapping. His eyes are fixed on Arlo who has moved to the front
to face him as he moves across the lines.*

Arlo: Good. Now, let's play it. The first note is a C then a D. No
    valves to start, then 1 and 3.

Liam listens and watches Arlo's valves as he demonstrates.

Arlo: Now your turn. I'll clap again, so that you get the rhythm
    right. 1, 2, 3, 4 . . .

*Liam attempts the two notes. Initially, the stepwise interval,
C to D, is not correct. He overpitches the second note playing
a G (on valves 1 and 3, which would also be correct for D). This
leads to Arlo remarking on the mistake, demonstrating again,
playing a correct and incorrect version, and asking Liam to explain
the difference. Eventually, Liam plays the notes correctly.*

Arlo: Well done. Let's do a bit more. Put your feet back on the first
    line. Remind me: How many side steps for the first two notes?

Liam: Two.

Arlo: Great.

They continue with the melody, bit by bit from its start. They shuttle between moving on the lines, discussing the durations and pitches, Arlo modelling, Liam repeating and discussion of correct and incorrect performances. Soon they have worked their way through the entire melody and made their way across the village hall.

Arlo: Let's get the music out and see what that looks like on paper.

Commentary: This lesson was multisensory, creative and, at first, intriguing for the student. It captured Liam's attention quickly. He enjoyed moving across the room as he navigated the graphic score. His visual sense and proprioception were engaged (that is, his body's sense of its position and movement in a physical space). The lines on the floor offered a point of interest to embed musical concepts (the note lengths and pitches) and acted as a superb aide memoire too. When his teacher clapped, Liam might not have been able to hear it so well, but he could use his vision to keep in time. The exercise was a way to include whole-body musical experiences, akin to eurythmics, within an instrumental lesson. The end of this teaching vignette clarified that this was not a replacement pedagogy, but supplementary to using stave notation.

Non-auditory sensations

All humans perceive sound through non-auditory channels. Musical vibrations are transmitted from the skin to the brain's auditory cortex via the nervous system.[18]

In an innovative research project from the University of Liverpool Acoustic Research Unit an assistive hardware device was developed for d/Deaf users who could feel musical

---

18 see e.g., Hopkins, Maté-Cid, Fulford, Seiffert & Ginsborg, 2016, 2023

vibrations from their instruments through the palms of their hands or the soles of their feet.[19] *This vibrotactile device was compatible with electric or electro-acoustic guitars, electronic keyboards, or any acoustic instrument that could be used with a microphone or pickup e.g., drums, violin or cello, etc.*

Another example of this cutaneous mechanism is the esteemed percussionist Evelyn Glennie who performs barefoot.

Visibility, modelling and gesture

The instrumental teacher's visibility, modelling practices and gesture are key. d/Deaf people depend on visual cues to perceive music[20] with facial expressions, body movements, gestures and visual representations of music paramount.[21] Within the teaching room, the instrumental educator therefore needs to be aware of his or her position (distance, location) and orientation (facing, facing away) when giving verbal directions, explaining or when embodying the music.[22] d/Deaf learners need to be able to see their teacher, including those who lipread. Teachers also need to be cognisant of whether the learner is looking. It is natural for instrumental teachers to move around their rooms too whether to pick up a piece of sheet music or to adjust another student's mouthpiece, etc. However, when there is a d/Deaf pupil in that lesson, self-awareness becomes more critical. Obstructions, for instance a music stand, can easily get in the way of sightlines. Moreover, the instrumental teacher's hand positions, bowing, posture, etc. need to be clearly visible to the learner for effective modelling. The importance of the learner's visual perception may sometimes be highly significant in establishing pulse, meter and rhythm. If deemed valuable by the learner, gestural representations (for example, conducting throughout a learner's performance) may also support

---

19 *Musical Vibrations*, 2024
20 Hatch, 2021; Jones, 2015; McCord & Fitzgerald, 2006; Schraer-Joiner, 2014; Sutela & Ahonen, 2024
21 Bang, 2009; Jones, 2015; Yennari, 2010   22 cf. Schraer-Joiner, 2014

keeping in time. Again, this is about multisensory learning, which involves engaging the visual sense in music.

Verbal and non-verbal communication

It is important to be careful with one's diction and pace.[23] Instrumental teachers may need to annunciate clearly and steadily with concise, relevant instructions. It may be wise to avoid shouting or whispering, which can make it harder for the d/Deaf learner due to the limits of their assistive devices. It is also a misconception that a raised voice is a helpful way to communicate. It can be embarrassing for d/Deaf people and makes lip reading harder. Furthermore, eye contact in conversations may be significant as non-verbal cues assist people to locate appropriate moments to speak. d/Deaf learners may also find it more difficult to interrupt conversations. Those who use sign language tend to wait for another person to stop signing before they start. Lip readers commonly only pay attention to one person at a time. They need to see what is being said.

Teaching case study – Matthew, Max, Henry and Tuan

Matthew visits a primary school each week to deliver brass lessons. He gives a group lesson lasting 20 minutes to three boys – Max, Henry and Tuan – who are in Year 6 (ages 10–11 years). Tuan wears hearing aids and relies on lip reading. An interpreter does not accompany him to the lessons. This is a mixed brass group. Max and Tuan are learning the cornet whereas Henry plays a trombone (reading in treble clef).

The only available space for this group lesson is the school's small library area adjacent to a classroom. It is dimly lit with a small window and only one of the ceiling lights is working. It is summer and, due to light streaming in through the window into their eyes, Matthew has partially pulled across its curtain. Matthew has collected the three high-spirited boys from the school playing field where they have been competing in their sports day. Matthew is

---

23 Schraer-Joiner, 2014

aware he needs to address the children's behaviour quickly before it derails the entire lesson.

Max (pupil): I beat you.
Henry (pupil): Nah, you're slow.
Max: Don't call me slow. You're the one who's stupid.
Matthew (teacher): Boys! Focus. Get your instruments out. (with a
    raised voice)
Tuan (pupil): I won my race.
Matthew: Everyone, pay attention! (raised voice)

The three boys stand in a row in front of a music stand with their instruments. Matthew stands alongside them.

Matthew: Let's play the first phrase together quietly like this.
    (whispering to gain the children's focus)
Max: You're slow Henry. You'll still be playing when we've finished.
    (overlapping his teacher's comment and whispering)
Matthew: Max, it isn't okay to talk like that. (interrupting Max with a
    raised voice)
Max: Sorry.
Matthew: Let's play it: 1, 2, 3, 4 . . .

The children play the phrase, which is marked pianissimo, *but noticeably Tuan's first few notes are much louder before he adjusts to the dynamic required.*

What went wrong? A combination of the children's high spirits, overlapping voices, the teacher position (alongside rather than in front and visible), and the physical space (dimly lit) made it difficult for Tuan to follow what was going on. It was understandable that he missed the instruction to play quietly. It might not have been possible to find a more suitable room. However, the lighting issues might be brought to the school's attention. Better positioning and more effective behaviour management, for example, allowing the group to settle before repeating instructions, might have led to an improved outcome.

Missed mistakes

Mistakes may be more easily missed by the d/Deaf learner. When a learner without a hearing disability makes a mistake, they hear it (being either conscious or unaware that it is an error). However, there is a greater chance that the d/Deaf learner has not heard it. The teacher might consider explaining, for example, "The third note, the crotchet, was too long" or "The highest note in that phrase, the C, was pitched too low" *subsequently* demonstrating the error by playing it. He or she might play correct and incorrect versions thereafter in a game whereby the student must identify the correct version. In that way, the teacher may be able to ascertain if the pupil is aware of the issue at hand.

Some considerations for the instrumental teacher
(interim summary):

- *Appreciate* the additional problems d/Deaf learners have with separating sound sources. Give verbal instructions separately from music that is being played. Ensure other learners in group lessons understand the protocols.
- *Set* audio device levels carefully.
- *Start* d/Deaf beginners with simple melodies before gradually adding polyphonic or textural complexity to repertoire over time. Duets, trios or backing tracks may be more troublesome due to complications with sound separation.
- *Use* music notation and/or other graphic representations of pitch and rhythm in the earliest stages of learning an instrument.
- *Orientate and position* yourself carefully when giving instructions. Notice any obstructions. Be aware that the pupil is looking.
- *Model* with hand positions, bowing, posture, etc. ensuring these are clearly visible.
- *Support* keeping in time with physical gestures (where appropriate).
- *Ensure* the d/Deaf disabled learner can see everyone in any group lessons or ensemble work.

- *Annunciate* clearly and steadily without shouting or whispering when giving instructions.
- *Explain then demonstrate* any errors the d/Deaf learner makes. Ask for identification of correct and incorrect teacher performances to test his or her perception and understanding.

Reflective questions

- What are the transferrable (non-musical) benefits for d/Deaf children's development from learning an instrument?
- Which assistive technologies are available? What are their implications for sound perception and instrument selection?
- How might working with d/Deaf learners affect the teaching space and how people are arranged within it?
- How might the issue of sound separation affect lessons?

Suggested further reading

Cheng, W., & Horowitz, W. (2016). *Making music with hearing loss* (2nd ed.). Association of Adult Musicians with Hearing Loss. https://www.musicianswithhearingloss.org/wp/

Darrow, A.-A. (1989). Music and the hearing impaired: A review of the research with implications for music educators. *Update: Applications of Research in Music Education, 7*(2), 10–12.

Darrow, A.-A. (1993). The role of music in deaf culture: Implications for music educators. *Journal of Research in Music Education 1993, 41*(2), 93–110.

Gertner, A., & Schraer-Joiner, L. (2016). Music for children with hearing loss. In D. V. Blair, & K. A. McCord (Eds.), *Exceptional music pedagogy for children with exceptionalities: International perspectives* (Chapter 11). Oxford University Press.

Glennie, E. (1990). *Good vibrations: My autobiography*. Hutchinson.

Jones, J. B. (2015). Imagined hearing: Music-making in deaf culture. In B. Howe, S. Jensen-Moulton, N. Lerner, & J. Straus (Eds.), *The Oxford handbook of music and disability studies* (pp. 54–72). Oxford University Press.

Leigh, I. W., Andrews, J. F., Miller, C. A., & Wolsey, J.-L. A. (2023). *Deaf people and society: Psychological, sociological and educational perspectives*. Routledge.

Schraer-Joiner, L. (2014). *Music for children with hearing loss: A resource for parents and teachers*. Oxford University Press.

Silvestre, N., & Valero, J. (2005). Oral language acquisition by deaf pupils in primary education: Impact of musical education. *European Journal of Special Needs Education, 20*(2), 195–213.

6

Physical Disabilities

What are physical disabilities?

We all encounter physical challenges throughout our lives. As a small child learning a large, hefty instrument we may struggle lifting and holding it, maintaining the required posture, or with blowing it (if woodwind or brass). Children may break an arm necessitating stopping violin lessons to allow time to heal. Professional musicians and music teachers may encounter playing injuries too (including neck and back pain and repetitive strain injury) due to the toll of practice.[1] Our bodies inevitably deteriorate too, and in old age we are likely to experience difficulties with manipulating objects, declining strength and with daily living and mobility. For the purposes of this chapter, 'physical disabilities' concern those that have significant and often longer-term impacts that are insurmountable through physical growth, commonplace adaptation, rest, normal healing or medical treatment. It is important to recognise that 'some people face more limitations than others and in ways that continuously affect their ability to participate in certain activities' (Culp & Jones, 2023, p. 42).

Physical disabilities result from illnesses, accidents, childbirth (defects and pregnancy complications), our genes and ageing. They can be congenital (at birth) or perinatal (occurring shortly afterwards), be inherent (associated with our genes) or acquired, have a slow onset or be sudden, and they can be degenerative. Physical disabilities can also involve conditions more immediately obvious, such as someone without a limb, or a wheelchair user, and those far less apparent. Physical disabilities can be musculoskeletal,[2]

---

1   see e.g., Crabb, 1980; Guptill, 2011, 2012; Guptill & Golem, 2008; Guptill, Zaza & Paul, 2005; Molsberger & Molsberger, 2012; Norris, 1996; Stanhope, Pisaniello & Weinstein, 2021
2 Eliassen, Trouli & Steder, 2024; Molsberger & Molsberger, 2012

including muscle weaknesses, brittle bones (such as osteogenesis imperfecta), poor or non-development of limbs (for example, due to thalidomide), or issues with a person's joints. A common example of the latter is rheumatoid arthritis, which is prevalent in the elderly. Neuromusculoskeletal disabilities[3] are specifically nervous system disorders (for example, with conditions such as cerebral palsy, spina bifida) and sometimes degenerative (such as, muscular dystrophy) so that a person's muscle control is impacted or they cannot move parts of their body well. These types of neurological difficulties can result from strokes, traumatic head or spinal cord injuries and genetics. Again, as with the other disabilities in this book, there is a vast range of circumstances, with these impacting music learning to different extents too.

The impacts on instrumental learning

> Throughout history, musical instruments have traditionally been designed for performers with a clear assumption in mind: every individual has two hands, ten fingers and equal functionality across those digits. This bias towards non-disabled performers has typically made certain instruments and musical styles inaccessible to musicians who do not satisfy these prescriptive criteria.[4]

The barriers to inclusion in instrumental music for those with physical disabilities come from instrument design, a rigid repertoire, preconceptions regarding what learners can achieve and lack of knowledge about available options.[5] This is a result of the traditions of music-making, its history and organisation, and society's associated values and expectations. This is particularly so with classical music due to its strict use of certain instruments, its fixed ensemble types and repertoire and how it is commonly learned and performed. 'Any deficiency or impairment in one hand or arm makes

---

3 Deepak & Ajeesh, 2012; Newitt, Barnett, & Crowe, 2015
4 Pearson, 2025, https://www.pearson.com/en-gb/schools/insights-and-events/schools-blog/2023/10/performance-and-physical-impairment-making-music-accessible.html
5 OHMI, 2025, https://www.ohmi.org.uk/; also read Vargas, 2020

traditional instruments unplayable to any reasonable standard. As a result, millions across the world are excluded from music-making for the lack of suitable instruments' (ibid.).

Similarly, novel instruments designed to be accessible may not easily fit within, for instance, the youth symphony orchestra. Yet, music educators today characteristically judge their role as producing inclusive environments and systems for learning.[6] This sets up significant decisions regarding physical disabilities and musical instruments: make do with what can be achieved on traditional ones such as those used in classical music or other more traditional genres; adapt these to make them more playable; or opt for novel, digital instruments designed specifically for disabled people, hybrid contexts and new music ensembles, etc. The latter might not be an inclusive route. This is picked up in the section below on instrument selection. Instrumental teachers may also simply be uninformed about adaptations that can be made – the easy and less specialist ones – due to their training and backgrounds.

A survey of 221 Nebraska high school music programmes by David Nabb and Emily Balcetis in 2010 found that 33 percent of the teachers involved were unaware that instruments could be adapted.[7]

Besides the traditions of music making, other influences on the instrument-learning process might be understood as concerned with the physically disabled learner: anatomy, strength and stamina, fine motor control and coordination, and tactile sensation. Table 13 offers some considerations. It is not intended to be exhaustive.

Benefits of learning an instrument

Many children and adults with physical disabilities encounter mental wellbeing issues from, as examples, social isolation, stigma and discrimination, or longstanding, chronic conditions causing

---

6 e.g., Bremmer, 2023; Darrow & Adamek 2018; Draper, 2024; Efstathiou & Varvarigou, 2025; Kruse, 2022; Liu, 2023; VanWeelden & Whipple, 2014; Walkup-Amos, 2020; Wong & Chik, 2015
7 *Nabb & Balcetis, 2010*

incessant pain. UK data from Census 2021[8] illustrated that disabled people had higher anxiety levels, lower life satisfaction and happiness, and considered their activities less worthwhile than non-disabled people. Musical participation and instrumental learning have great potential to engage physically disabled people in a meaningful, creative activity that combats loneliness, reduces anxiety and regulates mood. Playing the piano, for example, has been found to lower cortisol levels in learners thus decreasing anxiety.[9] Similarly, participants in group piano instruction have been compared with people who do not learn an instrument with the former experiencing decreased psychological distress, depression and fatigue.[10]

Instrument playing can build strength in the musculoskeletal and respiratory systems, improve circulation and fitness, and enhance a person's fine motor skills and hand-eye coordination. This applies to everyone. Research has ascertained that, after only four weeks of keyboard playing, learners with osteoarthritis had decreased pain in tandem with increased finger strength and dexterity.[11] Likewise, stroke survivors have seen improvements in dexterity and the coordination of their upper extremities after piano playing.[12] For stroke survivors '. . . this type of training [in people with neuromusculoskeletal disabilities] elicits a change in the reorganization of the sensorimotor cortex that results in improved movement quality'.[13] Naturally with age too, humans gradually lose function in their auditory system, cognition, memory and motor control. Some of this is a decline in the brain and nervous system. Debra Shipman (2016) notes that the brain:

> . . . works on a principle of 'use it or lose it.' . . . Brain plasticity is the ability of the brain to change its structure, and engaging older adults in sensory, cognitive, and motor activities creates positive outcomes. . . . Musical training provides a multisensory activity that requires integrating signals from different sensory modalities with motor responses.[14]

---

8 ONS, 2021   **9** Toyoshima, Fukui & Kuda, 2011
10 Seinfeld, Figueroa, Ortiz-Gill & Sanchez-Vives, 2013   **11** Zelazny, 2001
12 Villeneuve & Lamontagne, 2013
13 Rodriguez-Fornells, Rojo, Amengual, Ripollés, Altenmüller & Münte, 2012
14 Debra Shipman, 2016, https://pmc.ncbi.nlm.nih.gov/articles/PMC6368928/

Table 13. Considering physical disabilities and their effects on instrumental learning

	Questions	Effects and considerations
Anatomy	Is the condition e.g. neurological, or due to the poor development of a body part, or its absence?	Where e.g., limbs are missing, poorly developed or non-functional, many standard bilateral instruments (e.g. flute, trumpet, violin, cello, etc.) will be impractical without adaptations. Consider, for example, a guitar player with a missing hand due to thalidomide. Neurological conditions affecting movement and sensation may complicate playing certain traditional instruments due to the coordination and fine motor control typically required; in significant cases, a non-standard instrument might be more suitable.
	If a wheelchair user, are the upper limbs fully functional? What is the condition of the learner's respiratory system?	If the learner's upper body and respiratory system are fully functional, many standard instruments are playable. However, wheelchair users may experience challenges with travel to lessons and other musical experiences, or with access to buildings, etc.
Strength and stamina	Can the learner stand, or does he or she need to be seated to play?	
	Does the learner have enough strength and stamina (in the torso, limbs, fingers) to lift and maintain suitable posture with the instrument?	It is important to consider the size and weight of instruments selected, but also whether there are any adaptations that can be made (i.e., commercially available ones or specialist equipment) (see below).

	Will the learner's respiratory condition and embouchure allow for playing a wind instrument?	Where the respiratory system is weak, this may either rule out a standard wind instrument, or, if strong enough, could mean that learning one leads to potential health benefits.
Fine motor control and coordination	How will the learner's fine motor control and coordination affect playing?	Standard instruments require a high degree of fine motor control, physical coordination and dexterity. This applies across the human body in various ways, e.g., in the arms, hands and fingers for some instruments (e.g., the guitar, piano, violin) but also in the embouchure and tongue for others (e.g., trumpet, trombone, clarinet). The suitability of instruments will be associated with the nature of the learner's condition.
Sensation	Is there adequate sensation in e.g., the fingertips, etc.?	Where e.g., a guitarist is struggling to feel the fretboard, or a violinist to maintain a reasonable bow hold, it will be important to ponder ways to make the experience more tactile (see below) or, if too challenging, to opt for a different instrument.
Other	Are there any comorbidities to consider?	See elsewhere in this book for examples.

In summary, learning an instrument has weighty consequences for physical health both in disabled and non-disabled people. These include mental health and wellbeing gains (such as mood regulation, alleviating isolation and pain management), and physical wellbeing advantages (in developing and maintaining fine motor skills and bodily coordination, reducing fatigue, or through improved fitness, respiration and circulation).

Pedagogy

Instrument selection

The choice of a musical instrument for a physically disabled learner will be decidedly learner-centred, as much as physical disabilities are idiosyncratic. As explained above, selection may relate to the person's anatomy, strength and stamina, fine motor control and their capacities for coordination and receiving tactile sensations (such as in the fingertips for a pianist, violinist or guitarist). If we factor in comorbidities too, to include, for example, cognitive impairments or learning disabilities, then this becomes yet another consideration. We might divide the instruments available into three broad (non-exhaustive) categories of: standard instruments, specially adapted standard instruments sometimes with associated equipment, and novel, non-standard digital instruments designed for disabled people.

Standard instruments

Standard instruments are those commonly played by non-disabled people. These include those from longstanding Western and non-Western traditions, such as, the bassoon, cello, cornet, drumkit, electric guitar, euphonium, flute, French horn, oud, saxophone, shakuhachi, sitar, tabla, violin, etc. Some people with physical disabilities can and do learn these, either in a regular manner or with unconventional holding, posture or technique, or by means of commercially available enabling apparatus (such as stands, harnesses or simple additions to increase the tactile experience of the instrument) (see *Adaptions to standard instruments* below). Boyle and Widdison (2021) remark: 'Many instruments can be adapted to accommodate the needs of a particular player, and these should be explored before certain instruments are discarded as unsuitable for the individual'.[15]

Playing a standard instrument generally assumes that the person is bimanual (so can use both arms and hands), has enough upper body strength and coordination to lift the instrument and can maintain a suitable posture. There are smaller versions of instruments in some cases, for example, half-size guitars, violins, violas, celli and double basses, or mini bassoons. Lightweight plastic versions of some brass instruments also exist. Furthermore, commercially available stands and harnesses are available for some instruments such as the larger brass instruments (the baritone, euphonium and tuba) (see Table 15 below). Nonetheless, having enough respiratory condition is essential for playing wind or brass instruments. Woodwinds, for example, require sufficient air pressure and a strong embouchure.[16]

In addition, playing a standard instrument means that the learner must possess suitable fine motor skills, hand-eye coordination, dexterity and sensation in their fingertips (and, sometimes, their embouchure too), etc. Using self-adhesive dots or other labels may make an instrument more tactile by guiding the fingers. String teachers might also use bow guides. Instrumental teachers can be highly creative exploring with their students what works best. Inevitably, some instruments may be more suitable than others when considering the learner's physicality. Mara Culp and Sara Jones (2023) argue that the drum kit is well suited for learners with residual function in both their upper and lower extremities as it exercises coarse motor skills and coordination between the hands and feet. Whereas (ibid.) the piano is helpful for memory, timing and motor skills in the hands and arms. We are imagining a scenario here where the learner does not have significant comorbidities that get in the way.

Adapted standard instruments

Standard instruments have been adapted by specialist designers who are often involved with disability charities. Examples include

---

15 p. 97; cf. Zdzinski, 2001   16 Culp & Jones, 2023

one-handed versions of the flute, clarinet and saxophone that are playable by a person with a missing or non-functional arm or hand, and specially designed stands and mounts for instruments such as the trumpet or trombone which enable one-handed performance. The UK's OHMI Trust specialises in developing this type of instrument and associated equipment. Additionally, the trust offers an instrument hire scheme.[17] In the US in 2001, David Nabb launched a one-handed woodwinds programme at the University of Nebraska Kearney. He began teaching there with a Bundy prototype toggle-key saxophone created by Jeff Stelling.[18]

Adapted standard instruments are where we step into the realm of equipment designed specifically for the disabled user. Obtaining and utilising it relies on stakeholder disability organisations lending support to individual learners through their instrument hire schemes, development projects and other events. Since the intention is to make playing on standard instruments accessible, this has great potential. It can allow disabled learners to be included alongside non-disabled peers in group instrumental lessons or conventional ensembles (such as the school orchestra, the community wind band, etc.). Another upside is that the instrument being taught is familiar to teachers and is, therefore, within their experience, skills and knowledge. However, availability is a concern and costs may be high. Furthermore, playing an adapted instrument, as with all standard instruments, assumes that the disabled person has the bodily strength and coordination, fine motor skills and respiratory condition (if a blown instrument) to manage one.

Novel, non-standard instruments for disabled people

Novel, non-standard instruments have been produced. These typically leverage digital technologies. For instance, CMPSR ('composer') was created by the UK educational technology company Digit Music.[19] It is a hardware device with buttons to press that pairs with music software and its own app, Swipe. Those with restricted dexterity can play a collection of sounds including pianos, trombones and string sections. Soundbeam is another example. It

---

17 see OHMI, 2025 18 University of Nebraska Kearney, 2025 19 Digit Music, 2005

is a touch-free technology that uses sensors to translate physical gestures into sounds thus '. . .enabling people of all abilities to create music'.[20] These technologies are commercially available but, in some cases, may be cost-prohibitive for individuals and their families.

There have been projects leading to instrument designs for a specific musician's needs. These typically rely on enthusiasm and input from electronic engineers from the university sector allied to disability charities. Former professional orchestral trumpet player Clarence Adoo was paralysed below his shoulders due to an accident. Clarence now performs with Headspace, an electronic instrument producing digital sounds that are controlled by his head movements and a precise air column.[21] In another example, Drake Music UK[22] created the Kellycaster electric guitar for John Kelly, a disabled rock and pop musician. This has a short neck and interfaces with Ableton Digital Audio Workstation (DAW) software. It allows John to strum the strings normally with his right hand and select his chords by pressing a nearby controller keyboard with his left hand because it is not capable of manipulating the fretboard.

In the highly specialised world of accessible design, instruments, their technique and creative possibilities may look somewhat unfamiliar to most instrumental teachers. It is a world, too, where a decision has been made that standard instruments are intensely challenging or, indeed, impossible due to the severity of the learner's health situation. Instruments are sometimes, *but not always*, also created with severe comorbidities in mind, such as significant cognitive impairments or learning disabilities, and for therapeutic settings.[23] A key point to consider is whether these instruments can lead people into inclusive musical experiences. Whilst a child learning a violin might reasonably perform classical music in his or her school orchestra, learning a non-standard instrument leads the person to hybrid or new music contexts, or potentially limits participation with others.

---

20 Soundbeam, 2005, https://www.soundbeam.co.uk/; Magee & Burland, 2008
21 Adoo, 2025   **22** Drake Music, 2005
23 Bunt, 2003; Ellis, 1995, 1997; Hahna et al., 2012; Partesotti, Peñalba & Manzolli, 2018; Ward, Davis & Bevan, 2019

Teaching case study – Charlotte and Evan

Charlotte and Evan are two students with Profound and Multiple Learning Difficulties (PMLDs) of 20 and 23 years of age respectively. They are non-verbal with visual impairments and severe physical disabilities. Evan is tactile defensive meaning he does not like to hold things. Charlotte lies in a special care bed and Evan is a wheelchair user. They are at a specialist college. Charlotte is relatively immobile and tends to hold her head fixed to one side. Evan is far more active with his head and shoulders. They access musical experiences by using Soundbeam.

As mentioned above, Soundbeam is a technology with ultrasonic sensors. These look somewhat like microphones held in microphone stands. The distance of a player's body part, e.g., an arm or his or her head, from these is measured by Soundbeam's software. The sensitivity is adjustable. In this way, players can play digital samples of different instruments with their less-restricted body movements and gestures, even very tiny ones. The technology also includes wireless switches – hardware boxes that trigger backing tracks, linked films or loops, for a more immersive experience.

One sensor is pointed towards Charlotte's head. As she moves it towards a central or forward-facing position and back again, a Middle Eastern mode is played on a flute sound. The backing track has already been triggered by her teacher and a video of camels and a desert is displayed on a nearby flatscreen television. Charlotte smiles enthusiastically as she moves her head back and forth launching the flute upwards and downwards in pitch. At the same time, Evan accompanies Charlotte by playing an oud sound with the other sensor and his head. He rocks back and forth in his wheelchair moving in time.

Commentary: This was a therapeutic application outside most instrumental teachers' experience, which underscored that even those with the most severe physical disabilities can gain from music. The technology engendered opportunities for creative expression and enjoyment in two students who, otherwise, would have been unable to hold or manipulate an instrument. There were also possible health benefits, particularly notable in Charlotte, as the activity encouraged movement in her head and neck. It also held potential for meaningful interaction between the two students. After all, they were incapable of any verbal communication.

Table 14 provides some considerations for the three instrument categories discussed.

Adaptations to standard instruments

Fortunately, adaptations can be made to standard instruments easily with equipment not designed specifically for disabled people. Devices are available from music retailers and some are cost effective. Examples are the harnesses used by players of the larger brass instruments in marching bands (such as the euphonium, tuba), straps, grips, supports, instrument stands, bow guides (e.g., for violin, cello), or the lightweight, smaller versions of instruments intended for younger children (like the mini bassoon, plastic versions of cornets and trumpets, etc.). Additionally, music teachers can get creative in finding ways to increase tactile experience for learners and aid their manipulation of instruments, for example, with silicone grips for guitar picks, tape on fingerboards, self-adhesive dots or by building up the grips on mallets and drumsticks, etc. They can also make the decision to accept non-typical holding of an instrument, or unusual posture or technique where required. Table 15 offers some possibilities stratified by instrument group.

Table 14. General considerations in instrument selection

	Detail	Inclusive/exclusive	Health examples *(assuming no comorbidities)*
Standard instruments	Performed in a typical manner or unorthodox holding and posture. Smaller Instruments (e.g. half size versions). Facilitated with commercially available enabling apparatus (e.g., stands, harnesses etc.	Potentially *inclusive*	Suitable upper body strength, fine motor control and sensivity in fingertips for the instrument, etc. Wheelchair user with normal upper body control playing e.g., the violin, tenor horn, piano, etc.
Adapted standard instruments	One-handed versions. Specially designed stands and mounts for one-handed performing	Potentially *inclusive*	Absence of a limb, but with appropriate physical and mental capacities.
Novel, non-standard instruments	Commercially available digital instruments for disabled people. Bespoke versions designed for individuals.	Potentially *exclusive*, i.e. learning contexts specific to disabled individuals and groups, partic-pation in hybrid or new music ensembles.	Severely impacted physical coordination, strength and fine motor control, etc. Paralysed from the neck down (or suitable for those with e.g., significant cognitive impairments and learning disabilities.

Table 15. Some adaptations that can be made to standard instruments

Item	Description
Woodwind	
Flute key plugs	These are made of plastic or cork and can assist those with fingering issues.
Flute or clarinet thumb rest	A thumb rest or cushion aids balancing the instrument.
Swan-neck head joint for the flute	This is an ergonomic design to reduce strain in the neck and shoulders.
Mini or junior bassoon	These are often made from plastic resin so are lighter and easier to manipulate.
One-handed ocarina	Ocarinas also come in a variety of shapes and sizes helpful for children with fine motor control issues.
Brass	
Lightweight plastic versions of instruments	Lightweight plastic instruments (e.g., the pCornet or pTrumpet) are lighter and easier to hold.
Operating piston valves with the left hand (cornet, trumpet)	Players of most brass instruments operate their valves with their right hand (apart from the French horn). Although unorthodox, switching this might be helpful for cornet or trumpet players struggling e.g., with motor control in that hand.
Single French horn	The double horn in F/B♭ is a heavier instrument. Single orchestral horns may be more accommodating for those struggling with supporting them and maintaining the playing posture required.
Trombone hand	These are used for the hand bearing the support weight of the instrument thus

	alleviating strain in the hand, arm and shoulder.
Trombone slide extender	Slide extenders may make reaching sixth and seventh positions easier.
Tenor horn, euphonium, baritone or tuba harnesses	These hold the instrument to the player's body by means of shoulder straps, thus distributing weight and easing balancing.
Tuba or euphonium stands	These remove the weight of the instrument from the player's lap.
Percussion	
Electronic drum kits, pads and tabletop drums	These may be helpful for learners with limited motion or strength. Some have sensitivity controls so that the physical power needed for acoustic counterparts is not required.
Mallet grips or straps	Straps can be added to mallets or handles built up with tape or foam for learners struggling to grip or frequently dropping them.
Piano or keyboard	
Playing with one hand	There are notable piano works for one hand, e.g., Ravel's Piano Concerto for the Left Hand (1929–30), Brahms's transcription of Bach's Partita in D minor (1877) or Scriabin's Prelude and Nocturne, Op. 9 (1895). Although repertoire is limited, the Associated Board of the Royal Schools of Music (ABRSM, 2024) now includes one-handed material in its syllabus.
Strings	
Tape on fingerboard	Positioning tape on the fingerboard of string instruments provides a tactile reference for finger placement. This may

	be helpful for those with impacted sensation in the fingertips (e.g., due to nerve damage).
Bow guides (i.e., for violin or cello)	These devices fit below the base the fingerboard, with a slot or guides that assist students with keeping their bow motion straight and correctly positioned on the strings. These can be beneficial for learners with fine motor control problems.
Guitar capo	For learners who are finding left hand (fretboard) dexterity challenging, a capo may help with playing in different keys.
Playing guitar on lap in horizontal orientation (sound hole up)	Experimenting with this may be worthwhile for students with limited hand strength or where the normal posture for the guitar is troublesome.
Silicone grips for guitar picks	These can help students who drop their pick or slip with it.

Teaching case study – Ruby and Asif

Asif has muscular dystrophy. He is a bright 13-year-old. He experiences weakness in his shoulders and arms. Asif is hugely passionate about drumming and pop music. His physiotherapist has advised that physical activity would be beneficial for muscle tone, and he should stretch to avoid scoliosis (curvature of the spine). Asif's drum teacher, Ruby, feels that learning an acoustic drum kit could be too demanding and thus discouraging. Lessons take place at Ruby's home and Asif's mother brings him there once a week.

Ruby has set up an electronic drum pad with a stool for Asif. Next to this, she has positioned her drum kit. Ruby has also taped polyethylene foam lagging to the handles of two drum sticks for Asif. She got this from a hardware store. This is normally used for insulating heating pipes. Ruby has also put a piece of coloured tape as a visual reference target on Asif's pad. The lesson consists of Asif copying patterns that Ruby plays on her snare, which they then work on against an audio recording of a pop track. Occasionally, she moves from her kit to manipulate Asif's arms.

Commentary*: Ruby was exploring an adaptation for Asif. Bulking up the handles of Asif's sticks may well have helped him grip them, but this must be carefully monitored. His sensory modalities were occupied by the reference on the pad (visual), mirroring the teacher and coordinating with the backing track (auditory), and Ruby moving his arms (tactile, kinaesthetic). There were important considerations ahead about whether and how the learning might lead onto a full kit.*

Some considerations for the instrumental teacher
(interim summary):

- *Understand* the nature of the student's condition first and foremost.
- *Ponder* how anatomy, strength, stamina, motor control and tactile sensation affect the suitability of instruments.
- *Consider* the consequences of any comorbidities.
- *Balance*, on one side, the learner struggling yet experiencing enjoyment, physical health gains and health maintenance effects and, on the other, overburdening him or her.
- *Contemplate* the three instrumental categories discussed (standard, adapted standard, and non-standard) to ascertain which is most appropriate for the learner.
- *Consider* how instrument choice, as described above, has ramifications for inclusion and lifelong music participation.
- *Explore* the ways in which standard instruments can be adapted (for holding and supporting them, increasing tactile experience, or assisting coordination and motor control, etc.).

An open-minded, flexible approach

Open-mindedness and flexible strategies that recognise learner agency are imperative. Instrumental teachers can often draw on their students' feedback on what is achievable, what works regarding specific instruments and adaptations, and how these fit within their long-term aims and aspirations. As with the other SEND types in this book, parents and other caregivers can be hugely supportive and are an immensely valuable resource[24] with parental involvement a known predictor of educational success in children with disabilities.[25]

> Teachers should consider that some children have lived a significant portion of, if not their entire, lives with their physicality and can offer important contributions about what has worked, how, and why. Children for whom their disability was more recently acquired (for example, a car accident) may have less experience with adaptations and may feel less comfortable taking a lead role. Whatever the case, children possess unique and valuable insights and have a right to offer opinions on issues that affect them.[26]

More time may also be needed for kinaesthetic memories to become established, that is, the procedural, automatic, technical aspects of instrumental playing. Patience may be an essential quality of the teacher. Since instrumental learning will be highly personalised to the individual and his or her physicality, agility and being capable of change when something is not working is essential.

Adapting materials

Where required, simplifying music parts for group work or ensembles may be a way to include students with physical disabilities in collaborations involving disabled and non-disabled learners. For

---

24 Azad & Mandell, 2017; Olsen & Clarke, 2022; Schraer-Joiner, 2014
25 Musendo et al., 2023   **26**   Culp & Jones, 2023, p. 30

example, the rhythmic complexity of, for example., a drum part can be pared down or a less taxing melodic part assigned or arranged. Inclusivity is the aim, provided the intention is to develop skills progressively over time and, moreover, this does not emphasise deficits and differences to the learner's embarrassment.

Monitoring and giving feedback

Attention to multimodal methods is equally pressing when supporting students with physical disabilities. *Tactile feedback* might mean manipulating students into the right playing position or guiding their movements. However, a clear explanation of the purpose and the learner's permission are needed in tandem with that of parents or other legal guardians. It is also important to scope what is a normal, acceptable practice with those in authority in formal learning contexts such as schools. During lessons, a good practice is always to remember to ask before, for example, gently lifting a trumpet player's elbow if dropping too close to his or her ribcage, or before proceeding to guide a string player's bowing arm, etc. *Visual feedback* might be offered with the use of a mirror – either a small one held up by the teacher so the learner can see him- or herself, or with a full-length type. Unless by special permission with, for example, parents or those in loco parentis in schools, it is inadvisable to make videos of children's incorrect posture or performing movements on a teacher's phone, etc. This has the potential to lead to misunderstandings. However, teachers might make videos of themselves demonstrating an issue to be sent for reference during home practice if agreed. Adult learners do not present these risks.

Auditory feedback on physical position, movement, momentum and energy, etc. might be given both with positive remarks and formative, corrective points. Examples could be 'Dig in a little more on that downbow' or 'Exhale more forcefully and consistently into the mouthpiece'. Progress during lessons can easily slip during home practice. Parents may play a pivotal role in their child's educational or musical success.[27] Where parents can be encouraged to attend

---

27 e.g., Creech & Hallam, 2003; Macmillan, 2004; Rogers et al., 2009; Zdzinski, 1992, 1996

lessons, that has promise for effective monitoring and progress maintenance between them. Although this may be helpful for younger students, as borne out by, for example, the Suzuki method,[28] teachers should gauge if parental involvement (during lessons, at home) motivates. Some teenagers may find this demotivating.

Teaching case study – Finlay and Elizabeth

Elizabeth is an adult music learner who has private flute lessons with Finlay. These occur once a week at Elizabeth's home. She is an advanced flautist. Elizabeth developed Guillain-Barré syndrome two years ago after a serious respiratory infection. Her symptoms include general muscle weakness and difficulty walking. She currently sits for her lessons.

Elizabeth's neck tends to droop to the right as she plays. Finlay has noticed this issue with her posture and has brought a hand-held mirror to the lesson. He holds this so that Elizabeth can see what is happening. They discuss better posture, and Elizabeth suggests practising during the week in her bedroom, which has a long dressing mirror she can use.

Reflective questions

- What categories of physical disability are there?
- How do they affect instrumental learning?
- Which instrument types and adaptations are available? What are their connotations for lifelong engagement in music?
- How might the standard instrument you play be adapted?

---

28 Akutsu, 2019; Suzuki, 1969, 1987

Suggested further reading

Adoo, C. (2025, June 30). *Headspace*. The Clarence Adoo Trust. http://www.clarenceadoo.co.uk/headspace.html#

Culp, M. E., & Jones, S. K. (2023). Creativity is instrumental: Instrument-specific strategies and suggestions for assisting learners with physical disabilities and differences in general and instrumental music. *Music Educators Journal, 110*(1), 11–53.

Kinsella, V., Fautley, M., Nenadic, & Whittaker, A. (2018). *OHMI: Enabling music-making for the physically disabled (independent evaluation)*. Centre for Research in Music Education, Birmingham City University. https://www.ohmi.org.uk/teaching-research.html

Ciufo, T., Dvorak, A. L., Haaheim, K., Hurst, J., IONE, Leu, G. S., Miller, L., Mizumura-Pence, R., Oddy, N., Stewart, J., Sullivan, J., Tucker, S., Waterman, E., & Wilks, R. (2024). *Improvising across abilities: Pauline Oliveros and the Adaptive Use Musical Instrument*. University of Michigan Press.

Take It Away Consortium (Creative United, Drake Music, The OHMI Trust, Open Up Music and Youth Music UK). (2018). *Guide to buying adaptive musical instruments*. Creative United. https://takeitaway.org.uk/wp-content/uploads/2020/06/Guide-to-Buying-Adaptive-Musical-Instruments.pdf

7

Conclusions: Hallmarks of a Good Instrumental Teacher

The 'good' instrumental teacher

Writing this book has led the author to two fundamental questions:

- What makes a good instrumental teacher?
- Are the hallmarks different when that person embraces learners with Special Educational Needs and Disabilities (SEND)?

In this chapter, it is argued that, regardless of whom they teach, core hallmarks of good instrumental teachers are the same. So, unapologetically, this chapter offers some general, personal observations. Likely, there will be differing opinions on what 'good' entails with no list entirely exhaustive. Readers might notice that I do not judge instrumental teachers on pupil outcomes from external testing or examinations. This is because there are some aspects, for example, in the home, surrounding culture, and the pupil's wider life, etc. that are inevitably beyond the music educator's control. The hallmarks offered here are:

- having subject mastery
- being an advocate for music
- being an effective communicator and facilitator
- possessing a broad, inclusive view of music education
- agility in thinking, adaptability and responsiveness
- being a reflective practitioner
- appreciating one's positionality
- showing empathy
- and being someone who is clear and clearly organised

Subject mastery

Subject mastery must be considered *both* in terms of performing and teaching. Both are needed. Anecdotally, there is a pearl of wisdom circulating that 'an accomplished performer *does not* automatically constitute an effective teacher'. This is true for various reasons explored in this chapter. Those reasons are reinforced when we start considering SEND. However, that is not to suggest *in any way at all* that strong performance skills and their associated knowledge are somehow unnecessary for teaching an instrument. An instrumental teacher often needs to demonstrate, play alongside, interact musically with, and inspire his or her pupil. Where pedagogic knowledge and thinking are absent, poor teaching will ensue. Sadly, there is a hierarchy in the undergraduate music training of Western countries that prizes classical music performance and downplays the acquisition of pedagogic knowledge. Pedagogic knowledge is seen as optional, or the reserve of postgraduates. Musicians have also been found to esteem a performer identity above that of educator.[1] Yet, they typically have 'portfolio'[2] or 'Protean' careers,[3] with the latter named after Proteus who could change form at will. These include teaching roles. The 'system', therefore, leads some very skilled performers with little or no pedagogical training into teaching situations, sometimes with negative consequences. So, the first hallmark of a good instrumental teacher is that he or she has *both* performance and pedagogic capabilities.

An advocate for music

Good instrumental teachers understand the transformative power of music to enrich lives. Professor Susan Hallam's extensive review and synthesis of music education research, *The Power of Music*[4] has identified many ways in which this can happen. Her viewpoint is underpinned by extensive quantities of persuasive evidence. Music's power includes many identifiable benefits.

---

1 see Boyle, 2020; Mark, 1998; Mills, 2004b; Woodford, 2002; Triantafyllaki 2010
2 Boyle & Widdison, 2021   3 Bennett, 2008   4 2015; Hallam & Himonides, 2022

These include those relating to:

- aural perception, which in turn supports the development of language and literacy skills;
- enhanced verbal and visual memory skills;
- spatial reasoning which contributes to some elements of mathematics and constitutes part of measured intelligence;
- executive functioning which is implicated in intelligence and academic learning more generally;
- self-regulation which is implicated in all forms of learning requiring extensive practice;
- creativity, particularly where the musical activities are themselves creative; and
- academic attainment.[5]

Direct implications for those with SEND are threaded into the chapters of this book. Good instrumental teachers are advocates for music for all.[6] They speak out where this is not clearly understood by others (in schools, by policymakers, or by parents and other carers, etc.). They promote its worthiness as a positive activity for society, education and human development.

However, it is not just music engagement that brings profits. It is also its quality. Hallam (2015) also notes that the duration and intensity of training may be important, and there likely will be differences between individuals due to genetics.[7] Some studies also suggest that starting music training early in life is important.[8] So, there are contextual factors to reported advantages from musical participation.

An effective communicator and facilitator

A high-quality learning experience rests, e.g., on careful consideration of the teaching and assessment methods, and the resources used

---

5 Hallam, 2015, p. 103   6 Brenner, 2010   7 see e.g., Drayna et al., 2001
8 e.g., Amunts et al., 1997; Elbert et al., 1995; Lee, Chen & Schlaug, 2003; Li et al., 2010; Musacchia, Strait & Kraus, 2008; Ozturk et al., 2002; Pantev et al., 1998, 2001; Schlaug et al., 1995; Trainor, Desjardins & Rockel, 1999; Watanbe, Savion-Lemieux & Penhune, 2007; Wong et al., 2007

(scores, technologies), *but* it also relies on the interactions between participants. This book has explored some of the unique ways that people with SEND can apprehend and learn music, deploy assistive technologies and utilise adapted learning materials. However, it also highlighted that communication and interaction must be made specific to individuals. As one example, Chapter 1 called for reflection on appropriate terminology in relation to disability, that is, to understand the backcloth to people's lives and relate to them positively. Chapters 3 and 4, on autism and visual impairments, as just two other examples, illustrated how language and communication might be fashioned for specific learners. Communication has other foci too, such as giving formative advice effectively where needed and communication with parents. This means that good instrumental music teachers need to be effective, adaptable communicators. This is not just about what happens within the teaching room. Some teachers may move between educational contexts and must negotiate learning aims and processes with others, or, as mentioned above, advocate for music's significance. Furthermore, Hallam (2015) remarks that, in music groupwork, there must be social cohesion and inclusion, teamwork, empathy, psychological wellbeing and self-belief to realise the gains she notes (namely in language, literacy, spatial awareness, executive functioning, self-regulation and academic attainment). She writes:

> For these benefits to be realised the quality of the interpersonal interactions between participants and those facilitating the musical activities is crucial. The quality of the teaching, the extent to which individuals experience success, whether engaging with a particular type of music can be integrated with existing self-perceptions, and whether overall it is a positive experience will all contribute to whether there is a positive impact.[9]

So instrumental music teachers must also be successful facilitators. Everyone must be included and feel valued.

---

9 Hallam, 2015, pp. 104–105

A practitioner with a broad, inclusive educational perspective

Good instrumental teachers are passionate about their subject's potential regardless of each person's circumstances. They envision music as inherently human with instrumental learning a powerful contribution to a person's wider education. Any child or adult can engage in music and benefit. This is not *only* about technical skills, music reading, theory and playing repertoire well. Learning an instrument holds distinct qualities, for example, in the positive relationships and joy it generates, but also in its transferable attributes to other aspects of life, disciplines and areas. Instrumental learning can be about, just as a few examples: creativity, appreciating heritage, gaining cross-cultural awareness, citizenship, developing social skills, forging and sustaining friendships, pastoral support, health and wellbeing, learner confidence and sheer enjoyment. Good instrumental teachers understand how their work fits within this broader understanding of music education, which encompasses what happens *inside* schools and other formal institutions, but also *outside* them in informal learning[10] and in lifelong community music participation.[11] This may be because they have profited from participating in music themselves, often since childhood, in numerous ways and across various settings, such that music is a dominant thread in their identities. They understand that neurodiversity and disability are a normal part of the human spectrum as well (see Chapter 1). So, they have a perspective on music education that includes judiciously considering the inclusivity of their practices, modes of communication, learning materials, their surrounding policies, the contexts within which they operate and the physical environments in which they teach. They see ethical practice in fairness and respect for others as a foundational quality in their practice.[12] Kerry Boyle and Diane Widdison (2021) write:

> Inclusion in education is a pairing of the philosophy [of educational equality] and pedagogical practices that allows

---

10 Green, 2008; Hallam, Creech & McQueen, 2016
11 Bartleet & Higgins, 2018; Higgins, 2012, 2024; Roulston, 2010
12 Fernández & Martínez, 2022

each student to feel respected, confident and safe so that they can learn and develop to their full potential. It is a system of values and beliefs based on the best interest of the student that promotes social cohesion, belonging, active participation in learning, a complete education and positive interaction with peers. In an inclusive education, teachers value diversity and nurture the well-being and quality of learning from each of their students.[13]

Inevitably, this means having an overall moral position on education as inclusive practice, prioritising learner needs and being adaptable in approaches and aims. However, it also means appreciating one's limitations and, sometimes, finding a niche. After all, not all instrumental teachers are formally trained music therapists suitable for those with the most profound conditions and comorbidities. Understandably then, some instrumental teachers will decide to gravitate towards certain learner types. They may feel more comfortable teaching those who have less significant repercussions from their disabilities. That is fine. Other practitioners may sense their day-to-day life is becoming monotonous through lengthy experience, with their skillset lofty, thus comes a desire to diversify their client base with a new SEND specialism (see Chapter 1). Some of those practitioners might even pursue specialist training. Indeed, there are many possible scenarios. The terrain is richly varied, multi-layered, demanding and, therefore, fascinating. Whatever career path the good instrumental teacher chooses, however, and wherever he or she is on it, he or she will hold an inclusive vision as a member of a notable professional community.

Alas, research has shown educators draw on their own learning experiences to form teaching strategies,[14] may look to 'peak experiences' of being taught,[15] and some are '. . . learning alongside the children' (Baker, 2005a, p. 267). Instrumental performer-teachers are initiated into a culture of lengthy technical instruction ahead of any pedagogical training whereby '. . . individuals become immersed in "the traditions of the particular musicians who have

---

13 p. 93   **14** Baker, 2005a, b   **15** Mills & Smith, 2003

embraced this body of knowledge as a collective norm"'.[16] So, they naturally key into this, particularly in their earliest career stages as an educator. However, if they solely source ideas, values and standpoints from these remembered encounters, or from their role model teachers, this may be acutely problematic when they meet learners with SEND. There will be considerably different needs. It is a blunder to assume that the way one was taught in childhood will be motivational and effective for another or, indeed, for everyone. Instrumental teachers must be able to identify personal shortfalls, see merit in others' perspectives (including those of experts, specialists, caregivers and learners, etc.), and be open to personal transformation. They must not misconceive change as a threat to their existing practices, their musical histories and identities.

An agile thinker who is adaptable and responsive

Instrumental teachers need to be adaptable and responsive both to lesson situations, the wider circumstances in which they operate, and their students. They must be '. . . ready for the unexpected . . . [such that] the experienced teacher is armed with a range of activities and strategies that they can adapt to ensure that, whatever the situation, they deliver a musically enriching experience'.[17] Some of this is concerned with adjusting, such as to a student not arriving with his or her music book, or when a teaching room in a school is not available, but it is also about, for example, newly introduced technologies or changes to educational policy and its broader frameworks.[18] Instrumental teaching, whether involving disabled people or not, occurs in a context, whether that of a community music project, school, national educational system or internationally recognised examination board (e.g., the Associated Board of the Royal Schools of Music [ABRSM]). These contexts are not just physical spaces, but also about people's values, ideas and expectations, only some of which are formalised in policy documents or published curricula. Formal institutions such as special or mainstream schools, or specialist units within the latter, will also

---

16 Boyle, 2020, Ch. 1, p. 8   **17** Boyle & Widdison, 2021, p. 27   **18** Garet et al., 2001

possess teaching practice norms, typical beliefs in relation to them and surrounding policies. Good educators contribute positively to these institutional cultures.[19] Furthermore, where learners with SEND are verbal, communicative and able to articulate them, this can mean recognising how their musical interests can shape the learning process. Teachers who support student autonomy in a child-centred approach offer choices to enhance student wellbeing and motivation.[20] Keith Swanwick (2011) writes:

> Each student brings a realm of musical understanding into our educational institutions. We do not introduce them to music, they are already acquainted with it, though they may not have been subjected to the various forms of analysis that we may feel are important for their further development. We have to be aware of student achievement and autonomy, to respect what psychologist Jerome Bruner has called 'the natural energies that sustain spontaneous learning': curiosity; a desire to be competent; wanting to emulate others; a need for social interaction (p. 74).

If the instrumental teacher's position is totally averse to those of his or her learner, there will never be the highest quality motivation. If it is contrary to the people directly involved in his or her care, they, too, are unlikely to be supportive. So, good instrumental teachers must be agile enough as thinkers to adjust, but in countless ways.

A reflective practitioner

Someone who finds opportunities to reflect

Personal reflection can emanate from (as examples):

- Quietly mulling over lessons over a cup of tea or coffee
- Informal conversations about a student with other educators (e.g., in liminal spaces such as school corridors)

---

19 Fernández & Martínez, 2022 20 Bonneville-Roussy, Hruska & Trower, 2020

- Keeping teaching diaries and notes (on day-to-day teaching events or training to review development and inform progression)[21]
- Formal lesson planning (i.e., as part of it)
- Peer collaborations and mentoring
- Professional development events for the sharing of best practice
- Practitioner research (e.g., through reading, investigating on the internet, action research, etc.)

Staying up to date by engaging in opportunities for development is very helpful.[22] Kerry Boyle and Diane Widdison (2021) bid instrumental teachers to 'Keep learning: As musicians, we are constantly developing and adding to existing skills and abilities . . .'.[23] Regrettably, the role is sometimes isolated such as with practitioners working from their homes, and, sometimes, highly pressured, for example, with peripatetic teachers racing between school appointments. This makes it more difficult. Nonetheless, good practitioners recognise the centrality of discourse and reflection.

Reflective practice and action research

The term 'reflective practice'[24] is used in teacher development. This means having an awareness of one's positionality, showing empathy and perpetually engaging in critical self-examination of methods, personal values, decisions and learning outcomes, etc. There is no negative meaning to 'critical' here, which, instead, is oriented towards deep contemplation about oneself and one's actions for positive change in response to experiences and evidence. Reflective practice is particularly germane when working with music participants with SEND. Action research is one strategy for this.[25] It is a cyclical process of (i) identifying an issue or area for development in teaching and learning, (ii) deciding on

---

21 Boyle & Widdison, 2021

22 Fernández & Martínez, 2022; Lunenberg, Dengerink & Korthagen, 2014; Manfredo, 2008

23 p. 27   **24** Dewey, 1933; Schmidt, 2021; Schön, 1992

25 see Burwell & Shipton, 2013; Cain, 2008; Gaunt, 2007; Kemmis, Nixon & McTaggart, 2013; Mateos-Moreno, García-Perals & Maxwell, 2025; McNiff, 2013; Meissner, 2016; Mertler, 2019; Rumiantsev, 2024; Somekh, 2006

a definable change to one's practices (known as an 'intervention'), (iii) implementing it and (iv) gathering evidence of its impact, or otherwise, before (v) reflecting. That reflection leads to (ii) adjusting the existing intervention or starting again with a revised one, and thus the cycle continues. Figure 4 illustrates the process:

Figure 4. An action research cycle, adapted for instrumental teaching from McAteer (2013)

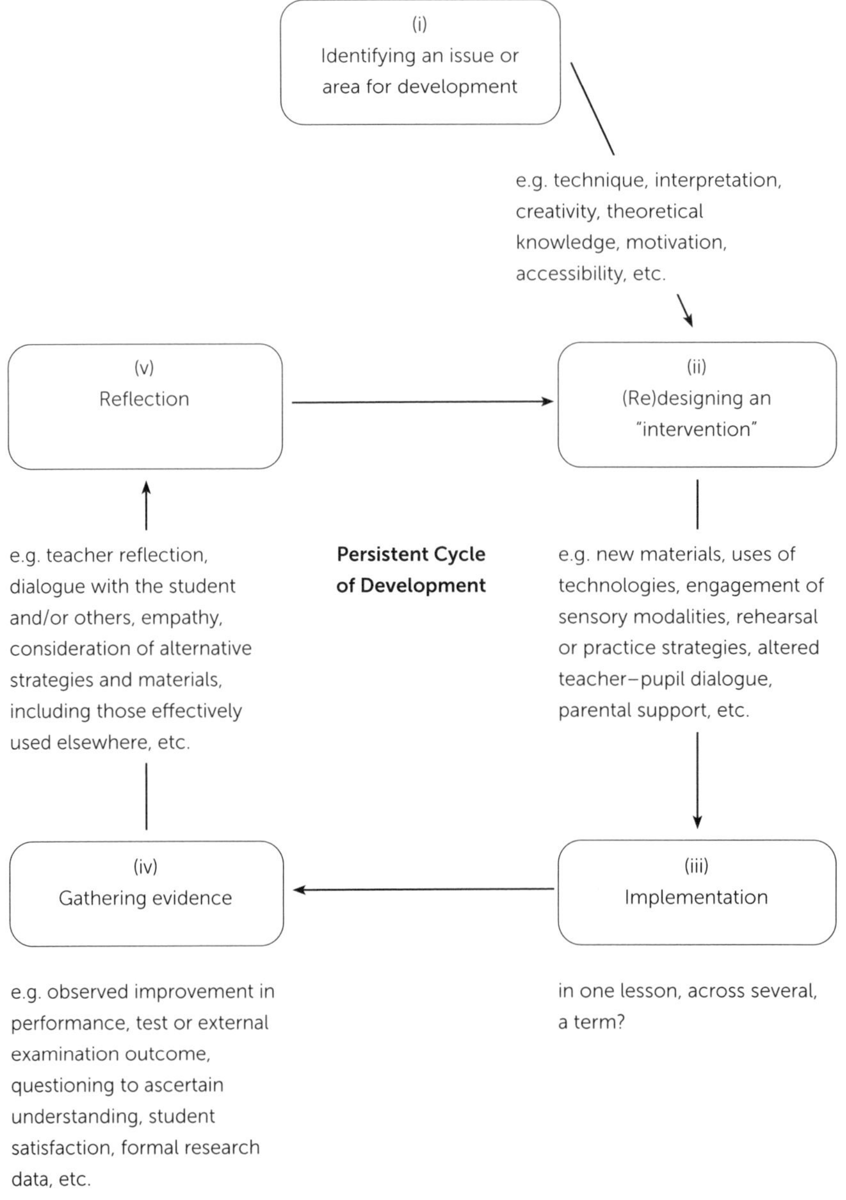

Teaching case study – Isla and Archie

Isla has been teaching 10-year-old Archie to play the oboe. Archie is doing well but she has noticed he panics when moving from the end of one stave system to the one below. There is always a disruptive pause. She reflects on Archie's dyslexia, his trouble with visual tracking and how he frustratedly says "the tiring part is where to go next". Isla decides to draw an arrow in pencil from the first system to the next to lead his eyes. She then observes the number of smooth transitions across the ensuing lesson. There is no improvement. Isla asks Archie about how he is approaching his reading and literacy more generally. She listens to Archie's account of his school's Special Educational Needs Co-ordinator (SENCo), Mrs Jones. Mrs Jones has been helping by marking asterisks in colour as well as arrows when he moves between paragraphs. Archie says he has found this helpful. Isla writes details of her ineffective strategy and Archie's comments about Mrs Jones in a teacher journal. She ponders this after the lesson. At the next lesson, Isla implements a similar system to that of Mrs Jones. She makes a mental calculation of the number of smooth stave transitions. This too, does not work. Isla decides they need to spend time getting Archie to memorise the first bar of the second system to assist his fluency.

Commentary: There were the seeds of an action research cycle. In the first cycle, Isla identified a problem: transitions between systems. She subsequently attempted a teaching 'intervention' by drawing arrows on the score, and she monitored the outcome. It did not help so she reflected. In a second cycle, Isla gained information on how Archie's reading at school was being supported to reframe her intervention. She implemented this by using colour and asterisks, and observed the outcome. Again, it did not work. Isla began a third cycle by attempting a new approach involving memorisation.

These cycles could continue, involving action, reflection and change, until the best approach for Archie is found. Approaches such as this could be upscaled into more formal action research, for example, by considering more concrete ways of measuring learning gains against a student's baseline capabilities and by formalising the process of teacher reflection.

Someone who considers his or her positionality

'Positionality' refers to self-awareness of how teaching and learning is shaped by one's background and subjectivities as an educator. Music teachers are in a powerful position in relation to their students. We all have predispositions about others whether we realise it or not.

In a landmark study, Harvard psychologist Robert Rosenthal and Principal Lenore Jacobson (1968) told teachers at a US elementary school that randomly selected pupils would be intellectual 'growth spurters'. That is, they had higher potential for academic achievement. Their study, Pygmalion in the classroom, *was named after George Bernard Shaw's play,* Pygmalion, *which was later the basis for Alan Jay Lerner and Frederick Loewe's musical,* My fair lady. *However, the children were randomly selected, not selected according to their track record of academic success or potential. The researchers then measured academic progress for all the children in the study. The supposed 'spurters' made greater progress than others. The investigators surmised this was due to greater investment in those children by the teachers including giving more instructional time in class, positive interactions with them, and, for example, not accepting poor responses to questioning. In short, the teachers' expectations for the students had influenced the learning outcomes.*

Likely, we all inadvertently engage in this process of 'labelling' our pupils.[26] There are other research studies, too, suggesting that teachers' expectations for learning and their learners hinge on their embedded judgments, often of which they are unaware, in relation

---

26 see e.g., Keddie, 1973

to different races, social classes and disabilities.[27] Therefore, we might also unintentionally do this with respect to SEND. It is easy to set low expectations, have preconceived notions about a singular 'right way' for these students musically, or have recourse to lore about them.[28] This may come from inexperience with 'setting the bar' appropriately, unfamiliarity with the alternatives, or a lack of awareness of accomplishments amongst those with SEND. Good instrumental teachers consider their positionality.

An empathiser

Small-group and one-to-one instrumental lessons can lead to close teacher-pupil relationships positively influencing learners' lives and futures. That naturally happens when, for example, teachers discuss pupils' musical interests and aspirations, or what is affecting practice time at home, the support they are getting, or their musical participation beyond lessons, etc. Awareness of students' emotional needs is crucial.[29] Paul Harris (2021) describes how we should notice subtle cues in our learners:

> . . . as teachers, we need to be strongly aware if we do lose our students' focus, attention and concentration; of if they are feeling uneasy or troubled by something we may have asked them to do. Changes in energy levels, tone of voice and facial expression can all be indicators of how our students are getting on. The quicker we can pick up the signals the quicker we can put things right and get back into the flow. Thus, through empathy we can become still more aware of our conditions and therefore more able to control them (p. 61).

Professional musicians often recognise role model teachers they encountered in their trajectories. They sometimes adopted a pastoral role well beyond *purely* helping them to play well. Accomplished performers, including internationally acclaimed soloists, have

---

27 e.g., Jones, 1972; Vulliamy, 1977a, b; Widayanti & Fletcher, 2022
28 Baker & Green, 2017; see Chapter 4   29 Bonneville-Roussy, Hruska & Trower, 2020

described their key teachers as being 'like having a second father' or as 'having maternal qualities'.[30] Those are perhaps bold examples, but many of us will recognise those who sought to empathise and guide. Empathy means being *aware* of, *sensitive* to, and *vicariously experiencing* the life and thoughts of another. It is part of the abovementioned broader perspective on music education and thus the teacher's role.[31] This also recognises how learning that occurs *inside* the teaching room is influenced by occurrences *outside* it and *vice versa*. Good instrumental teachers do not disregard this. They actively seek to understand their learners' lives. Students with SEND can have complex circumstances. If music educators only discuss the repertoire, technique, music theory, etc. required for 'passing the test', or if time pressures impinge on meaningful relationships and trust, they overlook their true potential.

Teaching case study – Veronica and Zahra

Veronica teaches the violin at a music conservatoire and is a professional orchestral musician. She has been waiting for Zahra to arrive for a consultation lesson to assess Zahra's capabilities and decide whether to accept her as a student. Unfortunately, without giving notice, Zahra is 20 minutes late for an hour-long session. Veronica is extremely irritated. Her other students always arrive on time. She is already tired after a long day and needs to leave promptly for a rehearsal.

Zahra is a wheelchair user. She first encountered issues with step-free access on her tube journey and had to rethink her journey. Zahra was flustered by this and found she had left her mobile at home. She is also neurodiverse affecting her personal organisation. On arrival at the conservatoire, the entrance was up a set of steps. The porter made her wait for a ramp and was unsympathetic despite Zahra's pleas to hurry, which led to an angry exchange. On arrival in the teaching room, Veronica's first words are "This isn't a good start" and "I'd expect better

---

30 interviews from Palmer & Baker, 2021
31 for discussions of empathy in education and music, see Davis, 2023; Goodrich, 2023; Sutherland, 1986

organisation from my pupils". Zahra was upset and this negatively impacted her performance in the lesson.

Commentary: There was a collision here. On one side of this, there was irritation at a perceived lack of respect for the teacher's status and circumstances and, on the other, Zahra's anger at how she had been treated coupled with embarrassment. It did not lead to a healthy, safe learning encounter at all. Perhaps both parties would have benefitted from greater empathy and understanding on both sides, before making negative assumptions.

Someone who is clear and clearly organised

Good instrumental teachers are clear, transparent and well organised with regards to matters that have been covered in this book. Amongst these are:

- SEND and its connotations for the learner (for lessons and life in general)
- Learner motivations, desires and concerns
- Accessibility matters (both within and beyond lessons)
- Appropriate learning materials, instrument adaptations and assistive technologies
- Suitable pedagogies
- Communication
- Policies and curricula in place
- Available support mechanisms
- The teacher's broader role
- Parents' and other caregivers' potential role in assisting
- Reflection as a means of personal development to enhance learning
- Aims, objectives and lesson planning

There are others. Certainly, an effective teacher is explicit about his or her aims and objectives. *Educational aims* are about overall intent. They give a sense of direction in the learning process. However, they do not detail precise short- or mid-term objectives that can be gauged as having been met or otherwise. An example aim for a cello student with a physical disability might be to 'Improve the learner's technical skills'. Another, for a blind guitar student, might be to 'Engage the learner in creativity'. By contrast, *objectives* pertain to aims; they are integral to them. They are more specific and action oriented. George Doran (1981) first coined the acronym SMART for objectives.[32] Objectives are:

- **S**pecific
- **M**easurable or, at least, patently observable
- **A**chievable
- **R**elevant
- **T**ime-bound

So, a corresponding objective for the cello student might be 'Remove the learner's bow guide from Term 2 after which the student will have achieved appropriate alignment'. This is: *specific* in outlining an action; *measurable* in that the outcome can be seen; deemed *achievable* by the teacher; *relevant* to the aim of improving bowing technique; and *time-bound* in desiring to have a positive outcome by the second term. An objective for the guitar student might be 'Create a 12-bar blues audio file by [a specified date] using a Digital Audio Workstation, assistive technologies and student improvisations'.

A note on lesson planning

Aims and objectives are essential in formal lesson planning such as in school-based teaching, work within music hubs, or within special educational sites. Independent practitioners can consider them too, even for planning and lesson contemplation in more casual forms. Planning can be long-range, mid-term (e.g., across several weeks or a term) or concerned with individual lessons, or combinations of these. Good instrumental teachers design curricula with sensible progression from foundational to advanced skills.[33]

---

32 also see Poe et al., 2021   33 Manfredo, 2008

A useful way to interpret planning though, is *not merely* as a description of what needs to be done in lessons (for example, a breakdown of tasks and pieces to be completed), but *also* a means to drive reflective practice and teacher development. Built into any paperwork might be a way for educators to record their thoughts on what had been effective, even sometimes unexpectedly, and thus worthwhile in response to a lesson or activity, and what had not. This self-monitoring can be formative and enrich learning. A reflective diary could be one solution.

Conclusions

At the start of this book, some challenges for the instrumental teacher were posited. These included gaining knowledge of suitable pedagogies and accessible learning materials, and the trials associated with acquiring the latter too. Music educators must also be able and willing to adapt their practices. Some can find this difficult to entertain, even threatening, due to their learning pathways and the educational culture they have inhabited. Another challenge mentioned was about identifying appropriate aims for students when SEND encompasses such an immeasurable array of potential conditions, comorbidities, learner experiences and desires. Moreover, that issue becomes further complicated when differentiating for diverse instrumental groups. Indeed, an inclusive educational paradigm warmly welcoming in those with alongside those *without* SEND is no easy feat. Then there are social barriers to break through including people's attitudes, conscious and unconscious bias, learner's fear of stigma and disclosure, and the learner's past experiences. The latter can lead to poor self-esteem and confidence, etc. The instrumental teacher sometimes works within constraints as well; perhaps those relating to a less-than-perfect, inaccessible physical space within a school for a particular student. There are many more hurdles and we could go on.

Although these challenges sound daunting initially, it is also from these that huge prospects for self-development and personal growth come, and for advocacy and enacting societal change too. The instrumental teacher can gain suitable pedagogical knowledge by reading books, investigating online, connecting with stakeholder organisations (see the *Directory* at the end of this book), reading research for an evidence-based position, enlisting in training opportunities, and by sharing with and learning from other practitioners. Moreover, he or she can use reflective practice and practitioner research to develop better ways of working. He or she can get to know the learner's circumstances, feelings and perspectives with empathy and care. Using these as a platform, he or she can break down social barriers and advocate for a more inclusive music education. The opportunities are endless. With this in mind, we would be wise not to underestimate the good instrumental teacher's power.

Reflective questions

- What are the hallmarks of a good instrumental teacher? What is accentuated when working with learners with SEND?
- How do the training routes of instrumental teachers serve as a platform for their pedagogical practices? What are the implications for their work?
- How might reflective practice be built into instrumental teaching?
- How might lesson planning be formed to feature aims, objectives and reflection?

Suggested further reading

Blair, V.-L., & McCord, K. A. (Eds.) (2016). *Exceptional music pedagogy for children with exceptionalities: International perspectives.* Oxford University Press.

Boyle, K. (2020). *The instrumental teacher: Autonomy, identity and the portfolio career in music.* Routledge.

Boyle, K., & Widdison, D. (2021). *Musicians who teach: A practical guide for instrumental and singing teachers.* Faber Music.

Burwell, K. (2012). *Studio based instrumental learning.* Ashgate.

Cain, T. (2008). The characteristics of action research in music education. *British Journal of Music Education, 25*(3), 283–313.

Hallam, S. (1998). *Instrumental teaching: A practical guide to better teaching and learning*. Heinemann.

Hallam, S. (2015). *The power of music: A research synthesis on the impact of actively making music on the intellectual, social and personal development of children and young people*. Institute of Education, University College London.

Harris, P. (2021). *Unconditional teaching: A ground-breaking journey towards a new style of music teaching*. Faber Music.

McAteer, M. (2013). *Action research in education*. Sage.

Mills, J. (2007). *Instrumental teaching*. Oxford University Press.

Mixon, K. (2007). *Reaching and teaching all instrumental students*. Rowman and Littlefield.

Pellegrino, K., Powell, B., & Hilliard, Q. (Eds.) (2023). *Teaching instrumental music: Contemporary perspectives and pedagogies*. Oxford University Press.

Somekh, B. (2006). *Action research: A methodology for change and development*. Open University Press.

Glossary of Terms

Ableism	Discrimination against disabled people, which can be due to conscious and/or unconscious bias. This manifests itself e.g., in the built environment, attitudes and expectations, policy, resourcing, education, access to musical experience, etc. that favour non-disabled people.
Action research (education)	An approach to practitioner research that aims to improve a specified aspect or aspects of the learning process through a cyclical process. Its cycle involves planning a change to practices (an 'intervention'), its implementation in lessons, data gathering and reflection.
Adapted instrument	A standard musical instrument that has been adapted for use by a player with special needs.
Additional need	In learning, e.g., an altered pedagogical approach, assessment mitigation, assistive technology, or extra resourcing, etc. required to make the learner's experience fair and equitable.
Assistive technology	A hardware or software technology for disabled people to facilitate daily living, computer access or music-making, etc.
Attention Deficit Hyperactivity Disorder (ADHD)	A condition characterised by inattention, hyperactivity and impulsivity that interferes with daily functioning and learning.
Autistic Spectrum	The medical name for autism. ASD represents a wide spectrum of neurological and developmental conditions that affect interaction with others, communication and learning in various ways.

Braille (music, literary)	A code used by some visually impaired people to convey language. This consists of cells of up to six dots that can be rendered on light card or presented on hardware devices (e.g., on a refreshable braille display). It is a code, not a language itself, so the term 'braille *translation*' is incorrect. Braille has has two forms: literary braille (for written text) and music braille.
Comorbidity/ comorbidities	The simultaneous occurrence of more than one health condition.
d/Deaf	'Deaf' (capital D) refers to people who have been pre-lingually deaf, i.e., with significantly impacted hearing at birth or before they learned to talk. These people generally use sign language as their first language and use Deaf to signify the unique culture to which they belong. In contrast, the term 'deaf' (lower case d) refers to anyone without much hearing, including those with hearing loss who do not sign and/or identify with the aforesaid culture.
Digital Audio Workstation (DAW)	A software application that functions as a virtual recording studio. Productions can be built by recording into it through microphones connected to audio interfaces by using MIDI devices, and with installed sample libraries and plugins. DAWs have a variety of editing facilities (also see 'MIDI').
Differentiation (in education)	Tailoring e.g., teaching practices and associated materials to meet the various requirements and learning styles within student groups, classes or other cohorts. This means going beyond a one-size-fits-all approach and acknowledging diversity.
Disability	This has been defined as a *biopsychosocial* condition resulting in restrictions in daily life, including e.g., inaccessible transport, buildings, experiences or education (see WHO, 2002 in this book). These

restrictions are connected to the person's *biological circumstances*, i.e., health and the body, *psychological effects* such as the person's confidence, identity and self-view, and *social conditions*, including others' attitudes, policy and associated funding mechanisms. Disability is a *normal* part of being human.

Dyslexia	This is a Specific Learning Difficulty (SpLD) that primarily affects reading and writing skills, including those involved in music (also see 'Specific Learning Difficulties').
Elementary school (US)	A formal educational site in US education for children from age 5 years (Kindergarten) normally to 10 years. It includes Grades 1 to 5. This progresses to Middle School (also known as Junior High School) for children 11 to 13 years (also see 'Primary school').
Equity (versus equality)	In education, the notion of differentiating e.g., pedagogical approaches, resourcing and other aspects of learning to make it fair for every learner. This contrasts 'equality' where every learner is given the same.
Formal learning	Learning that occurs in educational institutions, has a curriculum of content of increasing difficulty, involves direct teaching behaviours, is externally assessed i.e., by testing and an examiner, and is concerned with educational products or assessable outcomes (also see 'Informal learning').
High school (US)	A site in US education typically preceded by Junior High School/Middle School. This spans Grades 9 to 12, with students being of ages 14 to 18 years (with variations depending on state regulations). This is broadly equivalent to a UK secondary school (see 'Secondary school').

Inclusive practice (education)	Educational thinking and practices that value and seek to include all learners regardless of their circumstances. Thus, this brings learners together in experiences rather than siloing or marginalising individuals or learner types.
Informal learning	Learning that occurs anywhere, i.e., inside and outside educational institutions, has no curriculum, has no recognisable teacher role or entails facilitation or learning from peers, is internally assessed, e.g., through learner self-assessment or group assessment, may not be recognised by participants as learning, and is about educational process and experience (also see 'Formal learning').
Kinaesthesia	Awareness of the position and motion of the body by means of the proprioceptors in the muscles and joints (see 'Proprioception').
Large print (stave notation)	Stave notation that has been increased in size (also see 'Modified stave notation').
Learning disability	An intellectual disability significantly affecting learning. This is not to be confused with a 'learning difficulty' or 'Specific Learning Difficulty' whereby, with a suitably differentiated approach, the learner is potentially capable of typical or high attainment (also see 'Specific Learning Difficulty').
Medical model	Exclusive, ableist thinking that deems any problems encountered by the disabled person, educationally or more broadly, as the result of an abnormal body. The person's condition is to be cured or managed with no implication that society needs to change (also see 'Social model').
MIDI (Musical Instrument Digital Interface)	A digital communication protocol and language that allows electronic musical instruments, computers and other devices to communicate (also see 'DAW').

Modified stave notation	Stave notation with adjusted elements, e.g., by size, colour or spacing. Examples are coloured noteheads, an increased stave-line width, or altered paper colour (also see 'Large print [stave notation]').
Multisensory teaching and learning	Teaching and learning that engages the visual, auditory and kinaesthetic senses.
Neurodiversity	The broad spectrum of neurobiological (i.e., relating to the brain) and behavioural characteristics within the human population regarding e.g., cognition, sensory processing, motor abilities, social functioning, etc.
Participatory (versus presentational music)	Turino's (2008) conceptualisation of a type of music-making that involves group work, relies on improvised forms with no score, and thus no rehearsals ahead of performances, and brings together performers with diverse skillsets and backgrounds. Its improvised nature means the performers are the composers, rather than the performer and composer being separate with the former being the conduit of the revered composer. Its aims are inclusion and enjoyment through group interaction rather than technical competence at a valued, pre-determined repertoire. It, therefore, has various distinguishing features from the presentational music of the classical lens.
Person-first (versus identity-first language)	Terminology that, for political and advocacy reasons, places the person ahead of his or her disability, e.g., 'a person who is disabled' (rather than a 'disabled person').
Positionality	Acknowledgment of, and reflection on, biases we may have, hidden or overt, towards others. In education, this means teachers considering how

	their expectations for learners are shaped by their own backgrounds.
Primary school (UK)	A site for UK compulsory education for children aged 5 to 11 years. Primary schools often have a Reception class and what is known as Years 1 to 6. This is broadly equivalent to a US elementary school (see 'Elementary school').
Profound and Multiple Learning Disability (PMLD)	A significant learning disability alongside other disabilities impinging on a person's ability to communicate and live independently.
Proprioception	The body's sense of its orientation, position and movement in a physical space (also see 'Kinaesthesia').
Qualified Teacher of Children and Young People with Vision Impairment (QTVI)	A mandatory qualification for UK trained class teachers to specialise in teaching of pupils with visual impairments. This is approved by the UK's Department of Education. There are equivalent qualifications for other disabilities e.g., the Qualified Teacher of the Deaf (QToD).
Reflective practice	A process wherein teachers think critically about their experiences and practices to enhance teaching and learning outcomes. This involves self-awareness and development through experience, and it may involve practitioner research in educational contexts (also see 'Action research').
Secondary school (UK)	An educational institution in the UK providing compulsory education for students age 11 to 16 years (Years 7–11), or 11 to 18 years if it has a sixth form. Students complete Key Stages 3 and 4 culminating in national examinations (e.g., GCSE [General Certificate of Secondary Education]). This is broadly equivalent to a US high school (see 'High school').

Sensory impairment	An impairment to one of the human senses.
Severe Learning Disability (SLD)	A considerable intellectual disability affecting a person's capacity to learn new skills and manage daily life independently. This is neither to be confused with a 'learning *difficulty*' nor an 'SpLD'.
Social model (of disability)	Inclusive thinking that deems the problems encountered by the disabled person, educationally or more broadly, as the result of poor organisation by society. Issues can stem e.g., from unhelpful policy, negative attitudes, poor resourcing or the built environment, etc. This sees disability as part of the normal spectrum of humanity, not separate from it, and a positive identity. The implication is that society needs to change (also see 'Medical model').
Special Educational Needs (SEN)	A UK term applicable to learners with learning difficulties and disabilities who are identified as requiring additional support with their learning compared to peers. It is used in UK schools.
Special Educational Needs and Disabilities (SEND)	A term in widespread usage in the UK that encompasses learners with learning difficulties and disabilities. This is used in schools to refer to children who need additional support. Not all children with learning difficulties have a disability (see 'Specific Learning Difficulty').
Special Educational Needs Coordinator (SENCo)	A staff member role in a UK school, including in mainstream sites, responsible for overseeing the provision for students with Special Educational Needs and Disabilities (SEND).
Special school	A school designed exclusively for children with Special Educational Needs and Disabilities (SEND). This is where it has been determined that the children cannot best be served in the mainstream education

	system. These are schools with specialised support and facilities to address complex learning and developmental needs.
Specific Learning Difficulties (SpLD)	These are a set of diagnosable neurodiversity differences that affect individuals' information processing and learning. They include dyslexia, dyscalculia, dyspraxia, dysgraphia and ADHD (also see 'Dyslexia').
Talking score	An audio described version of stave notation.
Visual impairment	An umbrella term used in this book for the spectrum of people who are registered as blind or partially sighted. Some will have light perception, even functional vision, and some not.

Directory of Organisations

Name and contact details	Country	Priorities
Academy of Music for the Blind https://www.ouramb.org/	USA	Visually impaired young people and music
Amber Trust, The https://ambertrust.org/	UK	Visual impairment, children's music and instrumental learning, with a teacher directory including those offering music braille lessons at https://musicteacher directory.ambertrust.org/
American Music Therapy Association https://www.musictherapy.org/	USA	Music Therapy
Assistive Music Technology Lab for the Visually Impaired Department of Music Therapy, Berklee College of Music https://college.berklee.edu/ assistive-music-technology	USA	Music programme that prepares visually impaired students to use assistive music technologies, including digital audio production and music braille
Association of Adult Musicians with Hearing Loss https://www. musicianswithhearingloss. org/wp/	USA	Hearing loss and music
Associated Board of the Royal Schools of Music https://www. abrsm.org/en-gb/about-our- exams/specific-needs	UK	Instrumental examination board with a specific needs team that seeks to make reasonable adjustments

Name and contact details	*Country*	*Priorities*
Australian Music Therapy Association https://www.austmta.org.au/	Australia	Music therapy
Blind Citizens Australia https://www.bca.org.au/	Australia	Visual impairment
Blind and Low Vision Education Network New Zealand https:// www.blennz.school.nz/	New Zealand	Education network for visually impaired children that runs music courses
Blind Foundation, The https://blindlowvision.org.nz/	New Zealand	Music braille available
Blind Low Vision NZ https://blindlowvision.org.nz/	New Zealand	Visual impairment
British Dyslexia Association, The https://www.bdadyslexia. org.uk/	UK	People with dyslexia, including a music committee
British Performing Arts Medicine Trust https:// www.bapam.org.uk/	UK	Health and wellbeing services for the performing arts
Canadian Association of the Deaf (Association des Sourds du Canada) https://cad-asc.ca/	Canada	National organisation representing people who are d/Deaf
Canadian Association of Music Therapists https://www.musictherapy.ca/	Canada	Music therapy
Canadian National Institute for the Blind https://www.cnib.ca/	Canada	Visual impairment (the organisation also runs a music braille course)

Name and contact details	*Country*	*Priorities*
Children's Eye Foundation of AAPOS https://www. childrenseyefoundation. org/home	USA	Runs a programme called Vision Through Music in collaboration with The Academy of Music for the Blind
DAISY Consortium, The https://daisy.org/	Int.	Accessible file formats, technologies, training and development
Dancing Dots https:// www. dancingdots.com/	USA	Retailer of assistive music technologies for visually impaired people
Deaf Aotearoa https://www.deaf.org.nz/	New Zealand	National organisation representing people who are d/Deaf
Deaf Australia https://deafaustralia.org.au/	Australia	National organisation representing people who are d/Deaf
Drake Music https://www.drakemusic.org/	UK	Accessible music technology
Filomen M. D'Agostino Greenberg Music School https://fmdgmusicschool.org/	USA	Music education for people of all ages with visual impairments
Golden Chord c/o Connect Design https://www.golden-chord. com/	UK/Int.	Sells a back catalogue of music braille from its former transcription service, and has a directory of organisations worldwide offering music braille transcription or library services at https://www. golden-chord.com/braille-music-organisations.php

Name and contact details	*Country*	*Priorities*
Hearing Aids for Music School of Music, University of Leeds https://musicand hearingaids.org/	UK	Hearing aids for music, including advice and research
Help Musicians https://www.helpmusicians. org.uk/	UK	Physical and mental health support, including audiological assessments and custom-made hearing protection for musicians
Inner Vision Orchestra (Baluji Music Foundation) https://www.balujimusic foundation.org/inner-vision- orchestra	UK	Instrumental ensemble of blind musicians led by Baluji Shrivastav OBE
Interplay Orchestra, The https://www.interplay orchestra.org/	USA	Orchestra for adults with intellectual, developmental and other disabilities
Ivybridge Transcription Service Royal National Institute of Blind People https://personaltranscription. rnib.org.uk/Information/ AboutService	UK	Music transcription to accessible formats for the visually impaired
Jessie's Fund https://jessiesfund.org.uk/	UK	Charity supporting children with serious illness, complex needs, and communication difficulties through music
Lighthouse Guild https://lighthouseguild.org/	USA	Healthcare, support and training services for people with vision loss, including advice on music

Name and contact details	*Country*	*Priorities*
Musical Vibrations Acoustics Research Unit School of Architecture University of Liverpool https://www.musical vibrations.com/	UK	Vibrotactile research and development bringing music to d/Deaf people
Music and the Deaf https://www.matd.org.uk/	UK	Music making for people with hearing disabilities
Music Educators Network for the Visually Impaired (MENVI) https://www.menvi.org/	USA	Music braille available
Musicians Hearing Services https://www.musicians hearingservices.co.uk/	UK	Assessment of hearing issues, protection and hearing aids for musicians
Music of Life www.musicoflife.org.uk	UK	Charity providing music education and performance opportunities to children and young people with disabilities and special needs, including workshops in schools, music for d/Deaf children and one-to-one instrumental tuition
Music Therapy New Zealand https://www.musictherapy. org.nz/	New Zealand	Music Therapy
National Association of the Deaf https://www.nad.org/	USA	National organisation representing people who are d/Deaf
National Braille Press https://www.nbp.org/	USA	Press and braille advocacy organisation, including books on music

Name and contact details	Country	Priorities
National Deaf Center on Postsecondary Outcomes College of Education, The University of Texas at Austin https://national deafcenter.org/resource-items/music-classes/	USA	Offers music classes for learners who are d/Deaf
National Federation of the Blind https://nfb.org/	USA	NFB has a Blind Musicians Group and Performing Arts Division, and a summer children's residential course in music, Braille Beats (it also has a music braille course for teachers held at the University of Massachusetts, Boston)
National Library Service for the Blind and Print Disabled, The Library of Congress https://www.loc.gov/nls/services-and-resources/music-service-and-materials/	USA	Music braille resources
Nordoff Robbins https://www.nordoff-robbins.org.uk/	UK	Music therapy
OHMI Trust, The https://www.ohmi.org.uk/	UK	Accessible musical instruments
OmniMusic https://omnimusic.org.uk/	UK	Accessible music sessions using traditional and adapted instruments for disabled children and adults in partnership with local schools and community groups

Name and contact details	Country	Priorities
Paraorchestra https://paraorchestra.com/	UK	Instrumental ensemble comprising disabled and non-disabled musicians led by conductor Charles Hazlewood
Queensland Braille Writing Association https://www.braillehouse.org.au/	Australia	Music braille available
Royal National Institute of Blind People https://www.rnib.org.uk/	UK	Visual impairment, includes a music team, music library and transcription service for accessible formats (see Ivybridge)
Royal National Institute for Deaf People https://rnid.org.uk/	UK	National organisation representing people who are d/Deaf
Soundabout https://www.soundabout.org.uk/	UK	Charity concerned with music-making and training opportunities in relation to disabled people with complex needs
Sounds of Intent https://www.soundsofintent.org/	UK	Promotes the education of children and young people with complex needs in music
Sound Without Sight https://soundwithoutsight.org/	UK	Community-led initiative connecting blind and partially sighted performing musicians, audio engineers, and industry professionals to one another, and to resources, opportunities, and support

Name and contact details	Country	Priorities
Trinity College London https://www.trinitycollege.com/qualifications/music/special-needs	UK	Instrumental grade examination board that seeks to make reasonable adjustments
UNK One-Handed Woodwinds Program The University of Nebraska at Kearney https://www.unk.edu/academics/music/unk-one-handed-winds-program.php	USA	Develops one-handed woodwind instruments
Vancouver Adapted Music Society https://vams.org/	Canada	Supports and promotes musicians with disabilities, including an accessible recording studio, instrumental lessons, and instrument adaptations in partnership with Tetra Society of North America
Vision Australia Vision Library Service (VAILS) https://www.visionaustralia.org/	Australia	Music braille available
World Blind Union https://worldblindunion.org/	Int.	International organisation for the rights of visually impaired (blind and partially sighted) people
World Federation of Music Therapy https://www.wfmt.info/	Int.	Music therapy
World Federation of the Deaf https://wfdeaf.org/	Int.	International organisation for the rights of d/Deaf people

References

ABRSM (Associated Board of the Royal Schools of Music). (2024, June 29). *Explore piano music for one hand in our performance grades syllabus*. ABRSM. https://www.abrsm.org/en-gb/news/explore-piano-music-for-one-hand-in-our-performance-grades-syllabus

Accordino, R., Comer, R., & Heller, W. B. (2007). Searching for music's potential: A critical examination of research on music therapy with individuals with autism. *Research in Autism Spectrum Disorders, 1*(1), 101–115.

Adoo, C. (2025, June 30). *Headspace*. The Clarence Adoo Trust. http://www.clarenceadoo.co.uk/headspace.html#

Adreon, D., & Stella, J. (2001). Transition to middle and high school: Increasing the success of students with Asperger syndrome. *Intervention in School and Clinic, 36*(5), 265–279.

AFB (American Foundation for the Blind). (2025, June 30). *AFB: American Foundation for the Blind*. AFB. https://www.afb.org/

Akeroyd, M. A., & Munro, K. J. (2024). Population estimates of the number of adults in the UK with a hearing loss updated using 2021 and 2022 census data. *International Journal of Audiology*, *63*(9), 659–660.

Akutsu, T. (2019). Changes after Suzuki: A retrospective analysis and review of contemporary issues regarding the Suzuki Method in Japan. *International Journal of Music Education*, *38*(1), 18–35.

Alvares, G. (2019, July 11). *Why we should stop using the term "high functioning autism"*. Autism Awareness Australia. https://www.autismawareness.com.au/aupdate/why-we-should-stop-using-the-term-high-functioning-autism

AMB (Academy of Music for the Blind). (2025, June 30). *Make a difference in a blind child's life: Music is our vision*. AMB. https://www.ouramb.org/

American Psychiatric Association. (2013). *Diagnostic and statistical manual of mental disorders (DSM-5)* (5th ed.). American Psychiatric Association.

Amunts, K., Schlaug, G., Jäncke, L., Steinmetz, H., Schleicher, A., Dabringhaus, A., & Zilles, K. (1997). Motor cortex and hand motor skills:

Structural compliance in the human brain. *Human Brain Mapping, 5*(3), 206–215.

Azad, G., & Mandell, D. S. (2016). Concerns of parents and teachers of children with autism in elementary school. *Autism, 20*(4), 435–441.

Backhouse, G. (2001). A pianist's story. In T. R. Miles, & J. Westcombe (Eds.), *Music and dyslexia: Opening new doors* (Ch. 19). Whurr.

Bakan, M. (2020). *Music and autism: Speaking for ourselves.* Oxford University Press.

Baker, D. (2005a). Music service teachers' life histories in the United Kingdom with implications for practice. *International Journal of Music Education, 23*(3), 263–277.

Baker, D. (2005b). *Voices in concert: Life histories of peripatetic music teachers.* [Unpublished PhD thesis]. Institute of Education, Reading University.

Baker, D. (2013). Music, informal learning and the instrumental lesson: Teacher and student evaluations of the Ear Playing Project (EPP). In M. Stakelum (Ed.), *Developing the musician* (pp. 291–310. Ashgate.

Baker, D. (2021). Additional needs and disability in musical learning: Issues and pedagogical considerations. In A. Creech & D. Hodges (Eds.), *Routledge international handbook of music psychology in education and the community* (pp. 351–366). Routledge.

Baker, D., & Green, L. (2013). Ear playing and aural development in the instrumental lesson: Results from a "case-control" experiment. *Research Studies in Music Education, 35*(2), 1–19.

Baker, D., & Green, L. (2016). Perceptions of schooling, pedagogy and notation in the lives of visually impaired musicians. *Research Studies in Music Education, 38*(2), 193–219.

Baker, D., & Green, L. (2017). *Insights in sound: Visually impaired musicians' lives and learning.* Routledge.

Bang, C. (2009). A world of sound and music: Music therapy for deaf, hearing impaired and multi-handicapped children and adolescents. *Approaches: An Interdisciplinary Journal of Music Therapy, 1*(2), 93–103.

Baron-Cohen, S., Wheelwright, S., Skinner, R., Martin, J., & Clubley, E. (2001). The Autism Spectrum Quotient (AQ): Evidence from Asperger syndrome/high-functioning autism, males and females, scientists and mathematicians. *Journal of Autism and Developmental Disorders, 31*(1), 5–17.

Bartleet, B.-L., & Higgins, L. (Eds.) (2018). *The Oxford handbook of community music*. Oxford University Press.

Bashe, P., & Kirby, B. (2001). *The OASIS guide to Asperger syndrome*. Crown Publishers.

Batt-Rawden, K., & Denora, T. (2005). Music and informal learning in everyday life. *Music Education Research, 7*(3), 289–304.

BCA (Blind Citizens Australia). (2025, June 30). *Welcome to Blind Citizens Australia: Inform, connect, empower*. BCA. https://www.bca.org.au/

BDA (British Dyslexia Association). (2025, January 7). *Dyslexia*. BDA. https://www.bdadyslexia.org.uk/dyslexia

Bennett, D. (2008). *Understanding the classical music profession: The past, the present and strategies for the future*. Ashgate.

Blair, D. V., & McCord, K. A. (Eds.) (2016). *Exceptional music pedagogy for children with exceptionalities: International perspectives*. Oxford University Press.

Blind Low Vision NZ. (2025, June 30). *Blind Low Vision NZ*. BLVNZ. https://blindlowvision.org.nz/

Bonneville-Roussy, A., Hruska, E., & Trower, H. (2020). Teaching music to support students: How autonomy-supportive music teachers increase students' well-being. *Journal of Research in Music Education, 68*(1), 97–119.

Boyle, K. (2020). *The instrumental teacher: Autonomy, identity and the portfolio career in music*. Routledge.

Boyle, K., & Widdison, D. (2021). *The essential handbook for musicians who teach: A practical guide for instrumental and singing teachers*. Faber Music.

Braun, V., & Clarke, V. (2021). *Thematic analysis: A practical guide*. Sage.

Bremmer, M. (2023). Encountering disability in music: Exploring perceptions on inclusive music education in higher music education. *Research Studies in Music Education, 45*(3), 512–524.

Brenner, B. (2010). Reflecting on the rationales for string study in schools. *Philosophy of Music Education Review, 18*(1), 45–64.

Brimo, K., Dinkler, L., Gillberg, C., Lichtenstein, P., Lundström, S., & Åsberg Johnels, J. (2021). The co-occurrence of neurodevelopmental problems in dyslexia. *Dyslexia, 27*(3), 277–293.

British Academy of Audiology. (2024, January 14). *Positive terminology*. BAA. https://www.baaudiology.org/positive-terminology/

Brown, L. S., Draper, E. A., & Judith, J. A. (2022). Inside inclusive elementary music classrooms: Teachers and their students with Autism Spectrum Disorder. *Update: Applications of Research in Music Education, 41*(3), 48–56.

Bryant, P. E., & Bradley, L. (1985). *Children's reading problems*. Blackwell.

Bunt L. (2003). Music therapy with children: A complementary service to music education? *British Journal of Music Education, 20*(2), 179–195.

Burwell, K. (2012). *Studio based instrumental learning*. Ashgate.

Burwell, K., & Shipton, M. (2013). Strategic approaches to practice: An action research project. *British Journal of Music Education, 30*(3), 329–345.

Button, S. (2010). Music teachers' perceptions of effective teaching. *Bulletin of the Council for Research in Music Education, 183*, 25–38.

Cain, T. (2008). The characteristics of action research in music education. *British Journal of Music Education, 25*(3), 283–313.

Carlin, L. J. (2015). *Dyscalculia/dyslexia: Difficulties in sight-reading rhythm. Investigating the effectiveness of a new multi-sensory colour teaching intervention: Does it facilitate/improve SRRS?* [Unpublished MA dissertation]. Sheffield University.

Carrico, A., & Grennell, K. (2024). *Disability and accessibility in the music classroom: A teacher's guide*. Routledge.

Cheng, W., & Horowitz, W. (2016). *Making music with hearing loss* (2nd ed.). Association of Adult Musicians with Hearing Loss.

Cheng, X., Liu, Y., Shu, Y., Tao, D.-D., Wang, B., Yuan, Y., Galvin, J. J., Fu, Q. J., & Chen, B. (2018). Music training can improve music and speech perception in paediatric Mandarin-speaking cochlear implant users. *Trends in Hearing, 22*, 1–12.

Crichton, L. (1992). Music for everyone? *British Journal of Music Education, 9*(3), 211–215.

CNIB (Canadian National Institute for the Blind). (2025). *CNIB Foundation*. CNIB. https://www.cnib.ca

Crabb, D. J. M. (1980). Hand injuries in professional musicians: A report of six cases. *The Hand, 12*(2), 200–208.

Crankshaw, K. (2023, June 26). *Disability rates higher in rural areas than urban areas*. United States Census Bureau. https://www.census.gov/library/stories/2023/06/disability-rates-higher-in-rural-areas-than-urban-areas.html

Creech, A., & Hallam, S. (2003). Parent–teacher–pupil interactions in instrumental music tuition: A literature review. *British Journal of Music Education, 20*(1), 29–44.

Culp, M. E., & Jones, S. K. (2023). Creativity is instrumental: Instrument-specific strategies and suggestions for assisting learners with physical disabilities and differences in general and instrumental music. *Music Educators Journal, 110*(1), 41–53.

DAISY Consortium (2025, July 16). *The DAISY Consortium: Creating the best ways to read and publish*. The DAISY Consortium. https://daisy.org/

Darrow, A.-A. (1989). Music and the hearing impaired: A review of the research with implications for music educators. *Update: Applications of Research in Music Education, 7*(2), 10–12.

Darrow, A.-A. (1993). The role of music in deaf culture: Implications for music educators. *Journal of Research in Music Education, 41*(2), 93–110.

Darrow A.-A. (2003). Dealing with diversity: The inclusion of students with disabilities in music. *Research Studies in Music Education, 21*(1), 45–57.

Darrow, A.-A., & Adamek, M. (2018). Instructional strategies for the inclusive music classroom. *General Music Today, 31*(3), 61–65.

Darrow, A.-A., & Armstrong, T. (1999). Research on music and autism: Implications for music educators. *Update: Applications of Research in Music Education 18*(1), 15–20.

Daunt, S. (2012). *Music, other performing arts and dyslexia*. British Dyslexia Association.

Davis, T. (2023). Empathy and deep listening in jazz improvisation. In K. S. Hendricks (Ed.), *The Oxford handbook of care in music education* (pp. 205–216). Oxford University Press.

de Berruecos, P. V. (1967). Music for the deaf child. *International Audiology, 6*(2), 229–235.

Deepak, S., & Ajeesh, P. (2012). Development of a score for assessing severity, predicting interventions and prognosis of musculoskeletal disorders. *WORK: A Journal of Prevention, Assessment and Rehabilitation, 41*(S1), 6007–6010.

De Ferranti, H. (2009). *The last Biwa singer: A blind musician in history, imagination and performance*. Cornell University Press.

Dewey, J. (1933). *How we think: A restatement of the relation of reflective thinking to the educative process*. D. C. Heath.

Digit Music (2005). *CMPSR: Instantly Become a Musician*. Digit Music.
https://www.digitmusic.co.uk/cmpsr/

Disability Rights UK. (2024, October 18). *Social model of disability:
Language*. Disability Rights UK. https://www.disabilityrightsuk.org/social-
model-disability-language

Disability Wales. (2024, October 18). *Inclusive language and imagery*.
Anabledd Cymru. https://www.disabilitywales.org/socialmodel/inclusive
language-and-imagery/

Doran, G. T. (1981). There's a SMART way to write management's goals and
objectives. *Journal of Management Review, 70*(11), 35–36.

Drake Music (2005, February 15). *Drake Music*. Drake Music.
https://www.drakemusic.org/

Draper, E. A. (2020). Teaching students with Autism Spectrum Disorder:
Strategies for the music classroom. *General Music Today, 33*(2), 87–89.

Draper, E. A. (2024). Using technology to support students with disabilities
in inclusive music classrooms. *Journal of General Music Education, 37*(3),
39–41.

Drayna, D., Manichaikul, A., de Lange, M., Sneider, H., & Spector, T. (2001).
Genetic correlates of musical pitch recognition in humans. *Science, 291*,
1969–1972.

Dwyer, R. (2014). Future prospects for music education: Corroborating
informal learning pedagogy. *Music Education Research, 16*(2),
225–227.

Efstathiou, R., & Varvarigou, M. (2025). How inclusive are our music
classrooms? A theoretical model and case study from a preschool class
of a mainstream private nursery school in Cyprus. *Music Education
Research, 27*(2), 148–162.

Elbert, T., Pantev, C., Wienbruch, C., Rockstroh, B., & Taub, E. (1995).
Increased cortical representation of the fingers of the left hand in string
players. *Science, 270*, 305–307.

Eliassen, I., Trouli, H., & Steder, F. B. (2024). Prevalence of musculoskeletal
pain and associated factors among professional orchestra musicians in
Norway. *Scandinavian Journal of Public Health, 53*(4), 421–428.

Elliott, D. J. (1995). *Music matters: A new philosophy of music education*.
Oxford University Press.

Ellis, P. (1995). Incidental music: A case study in the development of sound
therapy. *British Journal of Music Education, 12*(1), 59–70.

Ellis, P. (1997) The music of sound: A new approach for children with severe and profound and multiple learning difficulties. *British Journal of Music Education, 14*(2), 173–186.

Fahey, J. D., & Birkenshaw, L. (1972). Education of the deaf bypassing the ear: The perception of music by feeling and touch. *Music Educators Journal, 58*(8), 44-51.

Fawcett, A. J., & Nicolson, R. I. (1995). Persistent deficits in motor skill of children with dyslexia. *Journal of Motor Behaviour, 27*(3), 235–240.

Fernández, M. P., & Martínez, J. F. (2022). Evaluating teacher performance and teaching effectiveness: Conceptual and methodological considerations. In J. Manzi, Y. Sun, & M. R. García (Eds.), *Teacher evaluation around the world: Teacher education, learning innovation and accountability* (pp. 39–70). Springer.

Flach, N., Timmermans, A., & Korpershoek, H. (2014). Effects of the design of written music on the readability for children with dyslexia. *International Journal of Music Education, 34*(2), 234–246.

Flick, U. (2022). *Doing interview research: An essential how to guide*. Sage.

FMDG (The Filomen M. D'Agostino Greenberg Music School). (2025, June 30). *The Filomen M. D'Agostino Greenberg Music School: Fostering education, access, and inclusion for people of all ages with vision loss*. FMDG. https://fmdgmusicschool.org/

Foster, P. (1996). *Observing schools: A methodological guide*. Sage.

Galaburda, A. M., & Kemper, T. L. (1979). Cytoarchitectonic abnormalities in developmental dyslexia: A case study. *Annals of the Neurology, 6*(2), 94–100.

Galaburda, A. M., Sherman, G. F., Rosen, G. D., Aboitiz, F., & Geschwind, N. (1985). Developmental dyslexia: Four consecutive patients with cortical anomalies. *Annals of Neurology, 18*(2), 222–233.

Galloway, H. F., & Bean, M. F. (1974). The effects of action songs on the development of body-image and body-part identification in hearing impaired preschool children. *Journal of Music Therapy, 11*, 125–134.

Ganschow, L., Lloyd-Jones, J., & Miles, T. R. (1994). Dyslexia and musical notation. *Annals of Dyslexia, 44*, 185–202.

Garet, M. S., Porter, A. C., Desimone, L. Birman, B. F., & Yoon, K. S. (2001). What makes professional development effective? Results from a national sample of teachers. *American Educational Research Journal, 38*(4), 915–945.

Gaunt, H. (2007). Learning and teaching breathing and oboe playing: Action research in a conservatoire. *British Journal of Music Education, 24*(2), 207–231.

Gertner, A., & Schraer-Joiner, L. (2016). Music for children with hearing loss. In D. V. Blair, & K. A. McCord (Eds.), *Exceptional music pedagogy for children with exceptionalities: International perspectives* (Chapter 11). Oxford University Press.

Gillberg, C. (2010). The ESSENCE in child psychiatry: Early symptomatic syndromes eliciting neurodevelopmental clinical examinations. *Research in Developmental Disabilities, 31*(6), 1543–1551.

Glennie, E. (1990). *Good vibrations: My autobiography*. Hutchinson.

Goodrich, A. (2023). Developing trust and empathy through peer mentoring in the music classroom. In K. S. Hendricks (Ed.), *The Oxford handbook of care in music education* (pp. 280–291). Oxford University Press.

Gouge, P. (1990). Music and profoundly deaf students. *British Journal of Music Education, 7*(3), 279–281.

Gov.UK. (2024a, June 6). *Academic year 2023/24: Schools, pupils and their characteristics*. UK Government. https://explore-education-statistics. service.gov.uk/find-statistics/school-pupils-and-their-characteristics

Gov.UK. (2024b, June 20). *Academic year 2023/24: Special educational needs in England*. UK Government. https://explore-education-statistics. service.gov.uk/find-statistics/special-educational-needs-in-england

Gov.UK. (2024c, October 26). *Data protection*. UK Government. https://www.gov.uk/data-protection

Gov.UK. (2024d, August 28). *Data protection in schools*. UK Government. https://www.gov.uk/guidance/data-protection-in-schools/data-processing-a-school-is-permitted-to-do

Gov.UK. (2024e, August 28). *Data protection in schools*. UK Government. https://www.gov.uk/guidance/data-protection-in-schools/what-data-protection-means-for-schools

Greasley, A., Crook, H., & Fulford, R. (2020). Music listening and hearing aids: Perspectives from audiologists and their patients. *International Journal of Audiology, 59*(9), 694–706.

Green, L. (2008). *Music, informal learning and the school: A new classroom pedagogy*. Ashgate.

Groemer, G. (2012). *The spirit of Tsugaru: Blind musicians, Tsugaru-jamisen and the folk music of northern Japan* (2nd ed.). Tsugaru Shobo Hirosaki.

Gubrium, J. F., Holstein, J. A., Marvasti, A. B., & McKinney, K. D. (Eds.) (2012). *The Sage handbook of interview research: The complexity of the craft* (2nd ed.). Sage.

Guptill, C. (2011). The lived experience of working as a musician with an injury. *WORK: A Journal of Prevention, Assessment and Rehabilitation, 40*(3), 269–280.

Guptill, C. (2012). Injured professional musicians and the complex relationship between occupation and health. *Journal of Occupational Science, 19*(3), 258–270.

Guptill, C., & Golem, M. B. (2008). Case study: Musicians' playing-related injuries. *WORK: A Journal of Prevention, Assessment and Rehabilitation, 30*(3), 307–310.

Guptill, C., Zaza, C., & Paul, S. (2005). Treatment preferences of injured college student musicians. *OTJR: Occupational Therapy Journal of Research, 25*(1), 4–8.

Hahna, N. D., Hadley, S., Miller, V. H., & Bonaventura, M. (2012). Music technology usage in music therapy: A survey of practice. *The Arts in Psychotherapy, 39*(5), 456–464.

Hallam, S. (1998). *Instrumental teaching: A practical guide to better teaching and learning*. Heinemann.

Hallam, S. (2015). *The power of music: A research synthesis on the impact of actively making music on the intellectual, social and personal development of children and young people*. Institute of Education, University College London.

Hallam, S., Creech, A., & McQueen, H. (2015). Teachers' perceptions of the impact on students of the Musical Futures approach. *Music Education Research, 19*(3), 263–275.

Hallam, S., Creech, A., & McQueen, H. (2016). Pupils' perceptions of informal learning in school music lessons. *Music Education Research, 20*(2), 213–230.

Hallam, S., & Himonides, E. (2022). *The power of music: An exploration of the evidence*. Open Book Publishers.

Hammel, A. M., & Hourigan, R. M. (2020). *Teaching music to students with autism* (2nd ed.). Oxford University Press.

Harris, P. (2015). *The virtuoso teacher*. Faber Music.

Harris, P. (2021). *Unconditional teaching: A ground-breaking journey towards a new style of music teaching*. Faber Music.

Hashemi, H., Pakzad, R., Yekta, A., Aghamirsalim, M., Pakbin, M., Ramin, S., Khabazkhoob, M. (2020). Global and regional prevalence of age-related cataract: A comprehensive systematic review and meta-analysis. *Eye, 34*(8), 1357–1370.

Hatch E. (2021). Performing without sound: Using sign language to teach expressive qualities of music. *Journal of General Music Education, 35*(1), 64–66.

Heikkila, E., & Knight, A. (2012). Inclusive music teaching strategies for elementary-age children with developmental dyslexia. *Music Educators Journal, 99*(1), 54–59.

Helps, S., Newsom-Davis, I. C., & Callias, M. (1999). Autism: The teacher's view. *Autism, 3*(3), 287–298.

Higgins, L. (2012). *Community music: In theory and practice*. Oxford University Press.

Higgins, L. (2024). *Thinking community music*. Oxford University Press.

Hoeft, F., Hernandez, A., McMillon, G., Taylor-Hill, H., Martindale, J. L., Meyler, A., Keller, T. A., Siok, W. T., Deutsch, G. K., Just, M. A., Whitfield-Gabrieli, S., & Gabrieli, J. D. E. (2006). Neural basis of dyslexia: A comparison between dyslexic and non-dyslexic children equated for reading ability. *Journal of Neuroscience, 26*(42), 10700–10708.

Holdhus, K., Murphy, R., & Espeland, M. I. (Eds.) (2021). *Music education as craft: Reframing theories and practices*. Springer.

Honeybourne, V. (2018). *The neurodiverse classroom: A teacher's guide to individual learning needs and how to meet them*. Jessica Kingsley.

Hopkins, C., Maté-Cid, S., Fulford, R., Seiffert, G., & Ginsborg, J. (2016). Vibrotactile presentation of musical notes to the glabrous skin for adults with normal hearing or a hearing impairment: Thresholds, dynamic range and high-frequency perception. *PLOS ONE, 11*, e0155807.

Hopkins, C., Maté-Cid, S., Fulford, R., Seiffert, G., & Ginsborg, J. (2023). Perception and learning of relative pitch by musicians with using the vibrotactile mode. *Musicae Scientiae, 27*(1), 3–26.

Hourigan, R. M., & Hammel, A. M. (2017). Understanding the mind of a student with autism in music class. *Music Educators Journal, 104*(2), 21–26.

Hourigan, R. M., & Hourigan, A. (2009). Teaching music to children with autism: Understandings and perspectives. *Music Educators Journal, 96*(1), 40–45.

Howe, M. J. A., & Sloboda, J. A. (1991). Young musicians' accounts of significant influences in their early lives. *British Journal of Music Education, 8*(1), 39–52.

Hsiao, F., & Gfeller, K. (2012). Music perception of cochlear implant recipients with implications for music instruction: A review of the literature. *Update: Applications of Research in Music Education, 30*(2), 5–10.

Hubicki, M. (2001). A multisensory approach to the teaching of musical notation. In T. Miles, & J. Westcombe (Eds.), *Music and dyslexia: Opening new doors* (pp. 85–100). Whurr.

Humphreys, P., Kaufmann, W. E., & Galaburda, A. M. (1990). Developmental dyslexia in women: Neuropathological findings in three patients. *Annals of Neurology, 28*(6), 727–738.

Hynd, G. W., Semrud-Clikeman, M., Lorys, A. R., Novey, E. S., & Eliopulos, D. (1990). Brain morphology in developmental dyslexia and attention deficit disorder/hyperactivity. *Archives of Neurology, 47*(8), 919–926.

Isaki, M. (1987). Japanese music and the blind. *British Journal of Visual Impairment, 5*(3), 103–105.

Jiménez, J., Olea, J., Torres, J., Alonso, I., Harder, D., & Fischer, K. (2009). Biography of Louis Braille and the invention of the braille alphabet. *Survey of Ophthalmology, 54*(1), 142–149.

Jones, J. B. (2015). Imagined hearing: Music-making in deaf culture. In B. Howe, S. Jensen-Moulton, N. Lerner, & J. Straus (Eds.), *The Oxford handbook of music and disability studies* (pp. 54–72). Oxford University Press.

Jones, R. L. (1972). Labels and stigma in special education. *Exceptional Children, 38*(7), 553–564.

Jorgensen, D. L. (1989). *Participant observation: A methodology for human studies*. Sage.

Jorgensen, D. L. (2020). *Principles, approaches and issues in participant observation*. Routledge.

Kaplan, B. J., Dewey, D. M., Crawford, S. G., & Wilson, B. N. (2001). The term comorbidity is of questionable value in reference to developmental disorders: Data and theory. *Journal of Learning Disabilities, 34*(6), 555–565.

Keddie, N. (1973). *Tinker, tailor: The myth of cultural deprivation*. Penguin.

Keil, S., & Clunies-Ross, S. (2002). *Teaching braille to children*. Royal National Institute of Blind People.

Kemmis, S., Nixon, R., & McTaggart, R. (2013). *The action research planner: Doing critical participatory action research*. Springer.

Kenny, L., Hattersley, C., Molins, B., Buckley, C., Povey, C., & Pellicano, E. (2016). Which terms should be used to describe autism? Perspectives from the UK autism community. *Autism, 20*(4), 442–462.

King, N., Horrocks, C., & Brooks, J. (2019). *Interviews in qualitative research* (2nd ed.). Sage.

Kinsella, V., Fautley, M., Nenadic, & Whittaker, A. (2018). *OHMI: Enabling music-making for the physically disabled (independent evaluation)*. Centre for Research in Music Education, Birmingham City University.

Kirk-Wade, E., Stiebahl, S., & Wong, H. (2024, March 17). *UK disability statistics: Prevalence and life experiences (research briefing)*. UK Parliament and House of Commons Library. https://commonslibrary. parliament.uk/research-briefings/cbp-9602/#:~:text=How%20many%20 people%20have%20a,24%25%20of%20the%20total%20population.

Kononenko, N. (1998). *Ukrainian minstrels: And the blind shall sing*. M. E. Sharpe.

Krolick, B. (1998). *How to read braille music: An introduction* (2nd ed.). Opus Technologies (National Braille Press).

Kruse, N. B. (2022). Equity in music education: Disrupting ageist ideologies through inclusive music-making. *Music Educators Journal, 109*(2),56–58.

Larsen, J. P., Hoien, T., Lundberg, I., & Odegaard, H. (1990). MRI evaluation of the size and symmetry of the planum temporale in adolescents with developmental dyslexia. *Brain and Language, 39*(2), 289–301.

Lebler, D. (2008). Popular music pedagogy: Peer learning in practice. *Music Education Research, 10*(2), 193–213.

Lee, D. J., Chen, Y., & Schlaug, G. (2003). Corpus callosum: Musician and gender effects. *Neuroreport, 14*(2), 205–209.

Leigh, I. W., Andrews, J. F., Miller, C. A., & Wolsey, J.-L. A. (2023). *Deaf people and society: Psychological, sociological and educational perspectives*. Routledge.

Lerner, N., & Straus, J. N. (2007). *Sounding off: Theorising disability in music*. Routledge.

Lisboa, T., Shaughnessy, C., Voyajolu, A., & Ockelford, A. (2021). Promoting the musical engagement of autistic children in the early years through a program of parental support: An ecological research study. *Music and Science, 4*, 1–24.

Li, S., Han, Y., Wang, D., Yang, H., Fan, Y., Lv, Y., Tang, H., Gong, Q., Zang, Y., & He, Y. (2010). Mapping surface variability of the central sulcus in musicians. *Cerebral Cortex, 20*(1), 25–33.

Liu, C.-W. (2023). Creating an inclusive music classroom. *Journal of General Music Education, 37*(2), 31–33.

Lubet, A. (2011). *Music, disability, and society*. Temple University Press.

Lunenberg, M., Dengerink, J., & Korthagen, F. (2014). *The professional teacher educator: Roles, behaviour, and professional development of teacher educators*. Springer.

Macmillan, J. (2004). Learning the piano: A study of attitudes to parental involvement. *British Journal of Music Education, 21*(3), 295–311.

Macmillan, J. (2008). Suzuki benefits for children with dyslexia. In T. Miles, J. Westcombe, & D. Ditchfield (Eds.), *Music and dyslexia: A positive approach* (pp 137–142). John Wiley and Sons.

Magee, W. L., & Burland, K. (2008). Using electronic music technologies in clinical practice: Opportunities, limitations and clinical indicators. *British Journal of Music Therapy, 22*(1), 3– 15.

Manfredo, J. (2008). Factors influencing curricular content for undergraduate instrumental conducting courses. *Bulletin of the Council for Research in Music Education, 175*, 43–57.

Mark, D. (1998). The music teacher's dilemma: Musician or teacher? *International Journal of Music Education, os-32*(1), 3–23.

Mateos-Moreno, D., García-Perals, J., & Maxwell, T. W. (2025). Teaching to practice productively and consciously: An action-research study in one-to-one instrumental music teaching. *Music Education Research, 27*(2), 203–214.

McAteer, M. (2013). *Action research in education*. Sage.

McCord, K., & Fitzgerald, M. (2006). Children with disabilities playing musical instruments. *Music Educators Journal, 92*(4), 46–52.

McNiff, J. (2013). *Action research: Principles and practices*. Taylor and Francis.

Meeker, N.-R. (2006). *Attitudes regarding blindness*. Musicians in Focus.

Meissner, H. (2016). Instrumental teachers' instructional strategies for facilitating children's learning of expressive music performance: An exploratory study. *International Journal of Music Education, 35*(1), 118–135.

Melago, K. A. (2014). Strategies for successfully teaching students with ADD or ADHD in instrumental lessons. *Music Educators Journal, 101*(2), 37–43.

Melcher, D., & Zampini, M. (2011). The sight and sound of music: Audiovisual interactions in science and the arts. In F. Bacci, & D. Melcher (Eds.), *Art and the senses* (pp. 265–292). Oxford University Press.

Mertler, C. A. (Ed.) (2019). *The Wiley handbook of action research in education*. Wiley-Blackwell.

Miles, T., Westcombe, J., & Ditchfield, D. (Eds.) (2008). *Music and dyslexia: A positive approach*. John Wiley and Sons.

Mills, J. (2004a). Conservatoire students as instrumental teachers. *Bulletin of the Council for Research in Music Education, 161/162*, 145–153.

Mills, J. (2004b). Working in music: Becoming a performer-teacher. *Music Education Research, 6*(3), 245–261.

Mills, J. (2007). *Instrumental teaching*. Oxford University Press.

Mills, J., & Smith, J. (2003). Teachers' beliefs about effective instrumental teaching in schools and Higher Education. *British Journal of Music Education, 20*(1), 5–27.

Mixon, K. (2007). *Reaching and teaching all instrumental students*. Rowman and Littlefield.

Molsberger, F., & Molsberger, A. (2012). Acupuncture in treatment of musculoskeletal disorders of orchestra musicians. *WORK: A Journal of Prevention, Assessment and Rehabilitation, 41*(1), 5–13.

Moreno, S., & O'Neal, C. (2000, May 11). *Tips for teaching high-functioning people with autism*. Indiana University Bloomington, Indiana Institute on Disability and Community, Indiana Resource Center for Autism. https://www.iidc.indiana.edu/irca/articles/tips-for-teaching-high-functioning-people-with-autism.html

Morris, M., & Smith, P. (2008). *Educational provision for blind and partially sighted children and young people in Britain, 2007*. Royal National Institute of Blind People.

Musacchia, G., Strait, D., & Kraus, N. (2008). Relationships between behaviour, brainstem and cortical encoding of seen and heard speech in musicians and nonmusicians. *Hearing Research, 241*(1–2), 34–42.

Musendo, D. J., Scherer, N., Jepkosgei, J., Maweu, L., Mupiwa, A., Hara, O., Polack, S., & Patel, D. (2023). A systematic review of interventions promoting parental involvement in the education of school-aged children with disabilities. *Australasian Journal of Special and Inclusive Education, 47*(2), 123–139.

Musical Vibrations. (2024, December 16). *What is Musical Vibrations?* Musical Vibrations. https://www.musicalvibrations.com/whatismusvib/

Myles, B., & Simpson, R. (2001). Understanding the hidden curriculum: An essential social skill for children and youth with Asperger syndrome. *Intervention in School and Clinic, 36*(5), 279–290.

Nabb, D., & Balcetis, E. (2010). Access to music education: Nebraska band directors' experiences and attitudes regarding students with physical disabilities. *Journal of Research in Music Education, 57*(4), 308–319.

Narita, F. M. (2015). Informal learning in action: The domains of music teaching and their pedagogic modes. *Music Education Research*, *19*(1), 29–41.

NCES (National Centre for Education Statistics). (2024, November 18). *Students with disabilities*. NCES. https://nces.ed.gov/programs/coe/indicator/cgg

Nelson, K. P., & Hourigan, R. M. (2016). A comparative case study of learning strategies and recommendations of five professional musicians with dyslexia. *Update: Applications of Research in Music Education, 35*(1), 54–65.

Newitt, R., Barnett, F., & Crowe, M. (2015). Understanding factors that influence participation in physical activity among people with a neuromusculoskeletal condition: A review of qualitative studies. *Disability and Rehabilitation, 38*(1), 1–10.

NHS (National Health Service). (2021, December 22). *Blindness and vision loss*. NHS. https://www.nhs.uk/conditions/vision-loss/

NHS. (2022, September 7). What is autism? NHS. https://www.nhs.uk/conditions/autism/what-is-autism/

Nordoff Robbins. (2025, April 24). *The Nordoff Robbins approach: Using the power of music to make a difference*. Nordoff Robbins. https://www.nordoff-robbins.org.uk/the-nordoff-robbins-approach/

Norris, R. N. (1996). Return to play after injury: Strategies to support a musician's recovery. *WORK: A Journal of Prevention, Assessment and Rehabilitation*, *7*(2), 89–93.

O'Brien, V. K. (2004). Adapting music instruction for students with dyslexia. *Music Educators Journal, 90*(5), 27–31.

Ockelford, A. (2000). Music in the education of children with Severe or Profound Learning Difficulties: Issues in current UK provision, a new conceptual framework, and proposals for research. *Psychology of Music, 28*(2), 197–217.

Ockelford, A. (2007). *In the key of genius: The extraordinary life of Derek Paravicini*. Hutchinson.

Ockelford, A. (2013). *Music, language and autism: Exceptional strategies for exceptional minds*. Jessica Kingsley.

Oglethorpe, S. M. (2002). *Instrumental music for dyslexics: A teaching handbook* (2nd ed.). Whurr.

Oglethorpe, S. M. (2008a). Can music lessons help the dyslexic learner? In T. Miles, J. Westcombe, & D. Ditchfield (Eds.), *Music and dyslexia: A positive approach* (pp. 57–67). John Wiley and Sons.

Oglethorpe, S. M. (2008b). Sight-reading. In T. Miles, J. Westcombe, & D. Ditchfield (Eds.), *Music and dyslexia: A positive approach* (pp. 82–91). John Wiley and Sons.

OHMI (One Handed Musical Instruments). (2025, June 30). *Music-making for people with physical disabilities*. OHMI. https://www.ohmi.org.uk/

Oleson, A., & Hora, M. T. (2014). Teaching the way they were taught? Revisiting the sources of teaching knowledge and the role of prior experience in shaping faculty teaching practices. *Higher Education, 68,* 29–45.

Oliver, M. (2009). *Understanding disability: From theory to practice*. Palgrave-Macmillan.

Olsen, R., & Clarke, H. (2022). *Parenting and disability: Disabled parents' experiences of raising children*. Bristol University Press.

ONS (Office for National Statistics, UK). (2021). *Outcomes or disabled people in the UK: 2021 (data and analysis from Census 2021)*. ONS. https://www.ons.gov.uk/peoplepopulationandcommunity/healthandsocialcare/disability/articles/outcomesfordisabledpeopleintheuk/2021

Ottenberg, S. (1996). *Seeing with music: The lives of three blind African musicians*. University of Washington Press.

Overy, K. (2000). Dyslexia, temporal processing and music: The potential of music as an early learning aid for dyslexic children. *Psychology of Music, 28*(2), 218–229.

Öztürk, A. H., Tasçioglu, B., Aktekin, M., Kurtoglu, Z., & Erden, I. (2002). Morphometric comparison of the human corpus callosum in professional musicians and non-musicians by using in vivo magnetic resonance imaging. *Journal of Neuroradiology, 29*(1), 29–34.

Palmer, R. C., & Ojala, S. (2022). Vibrational music therapy with D/deaf clients. *Voices: A World Forum for Music Therapy, 22*(3), 1–13.

Palmer, R. C., Skille, O., Lahtinen, R., & Ojala, S. (2017). Feeling vibrations from a hearing and dual-sensory impaired perspective. *Music and Medicine, 9*(3), 178–183.

Palmer, T., & Baker, D. (2021). Classical soloists' life histories and the music conservatoire. *International Journal of Music Education, 39*(2), 167–186.

Pantev, C., Engelien, A, Candia, V., & Elbert, T. (2001). Representational cortex in musicians: Plastic alterations in response to musical practice. *Annals of the New York Academy of Sciences, 930*, 300–314.

Pantev, C., Oostenveld, R., Engelien, A., Ross, B., Roberts, L. E., & Hoke, M. (1998). Increased auditory cortical representation in musicians. *Nature, 392*, 811–814.

Parbery-Clark, A., Strait, D. L., Anderson, S., Hittner, E., & Kraus, N. (2011). Musical experience and the aging auditory system: Implications for cognitive abilities and hearing speech in noise. *PloS ONE, 6*(5), e18082.

Park, H.-Y., & Kim, M.-J. (2014). Affordance of braille music as a mediational means: Significance and limitations. *British Journal of Music Education, 31*(2), 137–55.

Partesotti, E., Peñalba, A., & Manzolli, J. (2018). Digital instruments and their uses in music therapy. *Nordic Journal of Music Therapy, 27*(5), 399–418.

Pearson. (2025, June 30). *Performance and physical impairment: Making music accessible*. Pearson. https://www.pearson.com/en-gb/schools/insights-and-events/schools-blog/2023/10/performance-and-physical-impairment-making-music-accessible.html

Pellegrino, K., Powell, B., & Hilliard, Q. (Eds.) (2023). *Teaching instrumental music: Contemporary perspectives and pedagogies*. Oxford University Press.

Peterson, R. L., & Pennington, B. F. (2015). Developmental dyslexia. *Annual Review of Clinical Psychology, 11*, 283–307.

Pinto, D. (2014, January 20). Devoted to teaching music to the blind: Interview with David Pinto, Executive Director of Academy of Music for the Blind. *The Epoch Times*. http://www.theepochtimes.com/n2/arts-entertainment/blind-music-instruction-academy-david-pinto-26744.html

Poe, L. F., Brooks, N. G., Korzaan, M., Hulshult, A. R., & Woods, D. M. (2021). Promoting positive student outcomes: The use of reflection and planning activities with a growth mindset focus and SMART goals. *Information Systems Education Journal, 19*(4), 13–22.

Polischuk, D. K. (2016). Autism Spectrum Disorder research and its
implications for music teachers. *American Music Teacher, 66*(1), 15–18.

Reid, G., Fawcett, A., Manis, F., & Siegel, L. (2008). *The Sage handbook
of dyslexia*. Sage.

Reifinger, J. L. (2019). Dyslexia in the music classroom: A review of literature.
Update: Applications of Research in Music Education, 38(1), 9–17.

RNIB (Royal National Institute of Blind People). (2013). *Teaching music to
students with vision impairment (effective practice guide)*. Royal National
Institute of Blind People.

RNIB. (2025a, June 30). *Music Advisory Service and Transcription Service*.
RNIB. https://www.rnib.org.uk/living-with-sight-loss/independent-living/
reading-and-books/music-advisory-service-and-transcription-service/

RNIB. (2025b, June 30). *RNIB: See differently*. RNIB. https://www.rnib.org.uk/

Robbins, C., & Robbins, C. (1980). *Music for the hearing impaired*.
Magnamusic-Baton.

Rodgers, J., Glod, M., Connolly, B., & McConachie, H. (2012). The relationship
between anxiety and repetitive behaviours in autism spectrum disorder.
Journal of Autism and Developmental Disorders, 42, 2404–2409.

Rodriguez-Fornells, A., Rojo, N., Amengual, J. L., Ripollés, P., Altenmüller, E.,
& Münte, T. F. (2012). The involvement of audio-motor coupling in the
music-supported therapy applied to stroke patients. *Annals of the New
York Academy of Sciences, 1252*(1), 282–293.

Rogers, G. L. (1991). Effect of color-coded notation on music achievement
of elementary instrumental students. *Journal of Research in Music
Education, 39*(1), 64–73.

Rogers, M. A., Theule, J., Ryan, B. A., Adams, G. R., & Keating, L. (2009).
Parental involvement and children's school achievement: Evidence
for mediating processes. *Canadian Journal of School Psychology,
24*(1), 34–57.

Rose, J. (2009). *Identifying and teaching children and young people with
dyslexia and literacy difficulties: An independent report from Sir Jim Rose
to the Secretary of State for Children, Schools and Families*. The Dyslexia-
SpLD Trust. https://www.thedyslexia-spldtrust.org.uk/media/downloads/
inline/the-rose-report.1294933674.pdf

Rosenthal, R., & Jacobson, L. (1968). *Pygmalion in the classroom: Teacher
expectation and pupils' intellectual development*. Holt, Rinehart and
Winston Inc.

Roulston, K. (2010). 'There is no end to learning': Lifelong education and the joyful learner. *International Journal of Music Education, 28*(4), 341–352.

Rumiantsev, T., van der Rijst, R., Kuiper, W., Verhaar, A., & Admiraal, W. (2024). Teacher professional development and educational innovation through action research in conservatoire education in the Netherlands. *British Journal of Music Education, 41*(2), 195–208.

Schlaug, G., Jäncke, L., Huang, Y. X., Staiger, J. F., & Steinmetz, H. (1995). Increased corpus-callosum size in musicians. *Neuropsychologia, 33*(8), 1047–1055.

Schmidt, C. (2021). The reflective practices of early and late career music educators. *Research Studies in Music Education, 44*(1), 110–126.

Schön, D. A. (1992). *The reflective practitioner: How professionals think in action*. Routledge.

Schraer-Joiner, L. (2014). *Music for children with hearing loss: A resource for parents and teachers*. Oxford University Press.

Scott, S. (2017). *Music education for children with Autism Spectrum Disorder: A resource for teachers*. Oxford University Press.

Seinfield, S., Figueroa, H., Ortiz-Gil, J., & Sanchez-Vives, M. V. (2013). Effects of music learning and piano practice on cognitive function, mood and quality of life in older adults. *Frontiers in Psychology, 4*, 1–13.

Shaywitz, S. E., Shaywitz, B. A., Fletcher, J. M., & Escobar, M. D. (1990). Prevalence of reading disability in boys and girls: Results of the Connecticut Longitudinal Study. *Journal of the American Medical Association, 264*, 998–1002.

Shipman, D. (2016). A prescription for music lessons. *Federal Practitioner, 33*(2), 9–12.

SignHealth. (2024, December 6). *What is the difference between deaf and Deaf?* SignHealth. https://signhealth.org.uk/resources/learn-about-deafness/deaf-or-deaf/

Silvers, A., Wasserman, D., & Mahowald, M. B. (1998). *Disability, difference, discrimination: Perspectives on justice in bioethics and public policy*. Rowman and Littlefield.

Silvestre, N., & Valero, J. (2005). Oral language acquisition by deaf pupils in primary education: Impact of musical education. *European Journal of Special Needs Education, 20*(2), 195–213.

Silvestri, J. A., & Hartman, M. C. (2022). Inclusion and deaf and hard of hearing students: Finding asylum in the LRE. *Education Sciences, 12*(11), 773.

Smart, B., Peggs, K., & Burridge, J. (Eds.) (2013). *Observational methods*. Sage.

Snowling, M. (1997). *Dyslexia: A cognitive developmental perspective.* Blackwell.

Somekh, B. (2006). *Action research: A methodology for change and development*. Open University Press.

Soundbeam. (2005). *Soundbeam*. Soundbeam. https://www.soundbeam. co.uk/

Sounds of Intent. (2025). *Sounds of intent: An inclusive framework for musical engagement*. University of Roehampton, Trinity College London, Live Music Now and the Amber Trust. https://soundsofintent.org/en/ home/index

Spanner, H. V. (2023). *Lessons in braille music*. Hassell Street Press.

Stanhope, J., Pisaniello, D., & Weinstein, P. (2021). What do musicians think caused their musculoskeletal symptoms? *International Journal of Occupational Safety and Ergonomics, 28*(3), 1543–1551.

Stokes, M. A., Thomson, M., Macmillan, C. M., Pecora, L., Dymond, S. R., & Donaldson, E. (2017). Principals' and teachers' reports of successful teaching strategies with children with high-functioning Autism Spectrum Disorder. *Canadian Journal of School Psychology, 32*(3–4), 192–208.

Straus, J. N. (2011). *Extraordinary measures: Disability in music*. Oxford University Press.

Sutela, K., & Ahonen, O. (2024). 'I can feel the rhythm, and it is somehow nice': Deafness challenging the hierarchy of senses in music education. *Research Studies in Music Education,* https://doi.org/10.1177/1321103X231223864

Sutherland, M. B. (1986). Education and empathy. *British Journal of Educational Studies, 34*(2), 142–151.

Suzuki, S. (1969). *Nurtured by love: A new approach to education* (W. Suzuki, Trans.). Exposition Press.

Suzuki, S. (1987). Personalities in world music education. *International Journal of Music Education, os-10*(1), 36–38.

Swann, S., O'Brien, I., Rance, G., & Dowell, R. (2023). Interviews with musicians with hearing aids. *International Journal of Audiology, 63*(11), 844–852.

Swanwick, K. (2011). *Teaching music musically*. Routledge.

Take It Away Consortium (Creative United, Drake Music, The OHMI Trust, Open Up Music and Youth Music UK). (2018). *Guide to buying adaptive*

musical instruments. Creative United. https://takeitaway.org.uk/
wp-content/uploads/2020/06/Guide-to-Buying-Adaptive-Musical-
Instruments.pdf

Talking Scores (2025, February 6). *Talking scores: Making sheet music more
accessible for blind and print impaired musicians.* Talking Scores. https://
www.talkingscores.org/

Tallal, P., Miller, S. L., & Fitch, R. H. (1993). Neurobiological basis of speech:
A case of the pre-eminence of temporal processing. *Annals of the New
York Academy of Science, 682*(1), 27–47.

Tang, S. Y. (2025). An exploratory study of the experiences of musicians with
autistic traits in Higher Music Education in England. [Unpublished PhD
thesis]. University College London.

The Amber Trust. (2025, April 28). *The Amber Trust: Music for blind children.*
The Amber Trust. https://ambertrust.org/

TIMB (Toronto Institute of Music for the Blind). (2023, January 1).
Toronto Institute of Music for the Blind: Envision your voice. TIMB.
https://www.timb.ca/

Toyoshima, K., Fukui, H., & Kuda, K. (2011). Piano playing reduces stress more
than other creative activities. *International Journal of Music Education,
29*(3), 257–263.

Trainor, L. J., Desjardins, R. N., & Rockel, C. (1999). A comparison of contour and
interval processing in musicians and nonmusicians using event-related
potentials. *Australian Journal of Psychology, 51*(3), 147–153.

Triantafyllaki, A. (2010). Performance teachers' identity and professional
knowledge in advanced music teaching. *Music Education Research, 12*(1),
71–87.

Tunmer, W., & Greaney, K. (2010). Defining dyslexia. *Journal of Learning
Disabilities, 43*(3), 229–243.

Turino, T. (2008). *Music as social life: The politics of participation.* University
of Chicago Press.

UK Parliament. (2024, October 16). *Special education schools and colleges
in England: Policy and challenges in the special educational needs
sector.* House of Lords Library. https://lordslibrary.parliament.uk/
special-education-schools-and-colleges-in-england-policy-and-
challenges-in-the-special-educational-needs-sector/#:~:text=There%
20are%20around%20140%20post,the%202023%2F24%20academic%
20year

UN (United Nations). (2024, October 18). *Disability-inclusive language guidelines*. United Nations. https://www.ungeneva.org/sites/default/files/2021-01/Disability-Inclusive-Language-Guidelines.pdf

UNICEF (United Nations Children's Fund). (2021). *Seen, counted, included: Using data to shed light on the wellbeing of children with disabilities*. UNICEF.

University of Nebraska Kearney. (2025, May 13). UNK one handed woodwinds program. University of Nebraska Kearney. https://www.unk.edu/academics/music/unk-one-handed-winds-program.php

Vaiouli, P., & Andreou, G. (2018). Communication and language development of young children with autism: A review of research in music. *Communication Disorders Quarterly, 39*(2), 323–329.

Valle, J. W., & Connor, D. J. (2019). *Rethinking disability: A disability studies approach to inclusive practices*. Routledge.

Vance, K. O. (2004). Adapting music instruction for students with dyslexia. *Music Educators Journal, 90*(5), 2–72.

VanWeelden, K., & Whipple, J. (2014). Music educators' perceived effectiveness of inclusion. *Journal of Research in Music Education, 62*(2), 148–160.

Vargas, A. A. T. (2020). *Disability and music performance*. Routledge.

Villeneuve M., & Lamontagne, A. (2013). Playing piano can improve upper extremity function after stroke: Case studies. *Stroke Research and Treatment, 2013*, 1–5.

Voyajolu, A., & Ockelford, A. (2016). Sounds of Intent in the Early Years: A proposed framework of young children's musical development. *Research Studies in Music Education, 38*(1), 93–113.

Vulliamy, G. (1977a). *Music as a case study in the 'new sociology of education'*. Latimer.

Vulliamy, G. (1977b). Music as a case study in the 'new sociology of education'. In J. Shepherd, P. Virden, G. Vulliamy, & T. Wishart (Eds.), *Whose music? A sociology of musical languages* (pp. 179–200). Latimer.

Wald, M., & Bernstorf, E. (2024). Supporting autistic students and their siblings through inclusive music groups. *Music Educators Journal, 110*(4), 28–35.

Walkup-Amos, T. (2020). Creating inclusive music classrooms through peer-assisted learning strategies. *Teaching Exceptional Children, 52*(3), 138–146.

Wan, C. Y., Demaine, K., Zipse, L., Norton, A., & Schlang, G. (2010). From music making to speaking: Engaging the mirror neuron system in autism. *Brain Research Bulletin, 82*(3–4), 161–168.

Ward, A., Davis, T., & Bevan, A. (2019). Music technology and alternate controllers for clients with complex needs. *Music Therapy Perspectives, 37*(2), 151–168.

Watanabe, D., Savion-Lemieux, T., & Penhune, V. B. (2007). The effect of early musical training on adult motor performance: Evidence for a sensitive period in motor learning. *Brain and Cognition, 176*(2), 332–340.

Wearmouth, J. (2023). *Special Educational Needs and Disability: The basics*. Routledge.

Weiss, M. J., & Harris, S. L. (2001). Teaching social skills to people with autism. *Behaviour Modification, 25*(5), 785–802.

Welch, G. F., Ockelford, A., Carter, F.-C., & Zimmermann, S.-A. (2009). 'Sounds of Intent': Mapping musical behaviour and development in children and young people with complex needs. *Psychology of Music, 37*(3), 348–370.

Wengraf, T. (2001). *Qualitative research interviewing: Biographic narrative and semi-structured methods*. Sage.

Wesseling, L. (2004). *Focus on braille music*. Musicians in Focus.

WHO (World Health Organization). (2002). *Towards a common language for functioning, disability and health*. World Health Organization.

WHO. (2022). *Global report on health equity for persons with disabilities*. World Health Organization.

WHO (2024, February 2). *Deafness and hearing loss*. WHO. https://www.who.int/news-room/fact-sheets/detail/deafness-and-hearing-loss#:~:text=Deaf%20people%20mostly%20have%20profound,use%20sign%20language%20for%20communication.

Widayanti, C. G., & Fletcher, J. (2022). 'Everybody knows': Students labelled as having learning disabilities in the Indonesian education setting. *Education 3-13, 51*(8), 1354–1366.

Williams, H. (1989). The value of music to the deaf. *British Journal of Music Education, 6*(1), 81–98.

Williams, K. (2001). Understanding the student with Asperger syndrome: Guidelines for teachers. *Intervention in School and Clinic 36*(5), 287–298.

Williams, V. J., Juranek, J., Cirino, P., & Fletcher, J. M. (2018). Cortical thickness and local gyrification in children with developmental dyslexia. *Cerebral Cortex, 28*(3), 963–973.

Wisbey, A. S. (1980). *Learning through music*. M. T. P. Press.

Wong, M. W. Y, & Chik, M. P. Y. (2015). Teaching students with special educational needs in inclusive music classrooms: Experiences of music teachers in Hong Kong primary schools. *Music Education Research, 18*(2), 195–207.

Wong, P. C. M., Skoe, E., Russo, N. M., Dees, T., & Kraus, N. (2007). Musical experience shapes human brainstem encoding of linguistic pitch patterns. *Nature Neuroscience, 10*(4), 420–422.

Woodford, P. G. (2002). The social construction of music teacher identity in undergraduate music education majors. In R. Colwell, & C. Richardson (Eds.), *The new handbook of research on music teaching and learning* (pp. 675–694). Oxford University Press.

Yennari, M. (2010). Beginnings of song in young deaf children using cochlear implants: The song they move, the song they feel, the song they share. *Music Education Research, 12*(3), 281–297.

Zdzinski, S. F. (1992). Relationships among parental involvement, music aptitude, and musical achievement of instrumental music students. *Journal of Research in Music Education, 40*(2), 114–125.

Zdzinski, S. F. (1996). Parental involvement, selected student attributes, and learning outcomes in instrumental music. *Journal of Research in Music Education, 44*(1), 34–48.

Zdzinski, S. F. (2001). Instrumental music for special learners: By making minor adaptations, instrumental music teachers can find ways to include special learners in their classes. *Music Educators Journal, 87*(4), 27–63.

Zelazny, C. M. (2001). Therapeutic instrumental music playing in hand rehabilitation for older adults with osteoarthritis: Four case studies. *Journal of Music Therapy, 38*(2), 97–113.

Zimmermann, S.-A. (2005). Modified stave notation – encouraging musical independence through accessible, easily produced scores. *International Congress Series, 1282* (Vision 2005: International Congress, 4–7 April 2005, London, special issue, S. Jones, Ed.), 1113–1117.

About the Author

David Baker is Associate Professor at University College London (UCL), where he leads the Music Education MA, supervises PhD students, and has served as his department's Academic Head of Learning and Teaching. He is Fellow of the Higher Education Academy. His previous roles have been at Reading University and Trinity Laban Conservatoire of Music, London. In the wider Higher Education sector, David has assisted in developing new degree courses and modules across a range of education disciplines, and he has been External Assessor for periodic programme reviews, including at the Royal Academy of Music, London. David has also been External Examiner for PhDs in music education at universities and music conservatoires worldwide. His early background is as a peripatetic instrumental music teacher having taught in UK primary and secondary schools for over 10 years.

David has published research articles and book chapters on a wide variety of music education topics, including instrumental teaching, musical creativity, informal music learning and the lives of internationally renowned classical soloists. However, he has a particular interest in disability, music and assistive technology development, etc. He was Principal Investigator for 'Visually-impaired musicians' lives' (funded by the Arts and Humanities Research Council, 2013–15), which led to his co-authored book, *Insights in sound* (Routledge, 2017). That work has taken him as a presenter to Australia, India, Norway, Sweden and the USA.